DESIGN BEHIND DESIRE

Curated by Lisa Z. Morgan

Creative Direction by Susanne Schaal

Desire, as we know it, is a virtue and vice. I often wonder if our struggle with desire is what creates the energy of attraction towards it. The balancing of desire often seems like an impossible feat, yet wrestling with it is what makes it a force to be reckoned with. Desire as a vice can cause pain that brings endless nagging, which propels one into a state of continual unrest. It is addictive. I equally love desire for its virtuous qualities, how desire can tingle through our blood like popping bubbles inside our veins. The question for me has always been—how do we lead desire into the state of satisfaction instead of letting it fester in a bottomless pit of need?

My journey with objects of desire started at a young age, fed by my grandmother, a rebellious and disobedient Italian woman from a small southern town. She was a scandalous seductress and the first woman in her community to obtain a divorce. She used to sit me on her lap, feed me salami and cheese, and say, "Darling, always be desired but never possessed." My grandmother was an exceptional beauty and was courted by many men. She told me she learnt how to run fast so they could never catch her.

She was a true romantic with a tragic love story. She had a passion for social history and was a very entertaining storyteller. As a child I strained myself to try to imagine the smells and tastes of her childhood. She would say to me, "You will never be loved like I have been loved. Have you ever had a boy serenade you with a whole band before?"

It was my grandmother and her obsession with "pretty things" that taught me that beauty is the greatest of seductresses, "Darling, I only love beautiful things, nothing ugly, all I want to see is beauty."

I owe a lot to my grandmother, for my love of antiques comes from her. I will never forget when I was twelve, walking into the Victoria and Albert museum for the first time. I was shocked by my physical reaction to the beautifully crafted objects that sat so perfectly preserved behind museum cabinets. They gave me the same bubbling feeling that I had when I was falling in love or having a crush on a boy. It was then that I discovered it wasn't just beautiful objects that turned me on, but it was the mystery of the past, mixed with the unimaginable lost talent of the craftsmen that filled my favorite museum. Who were these men and women who carved, painted, wove and embroidered these exquisite pieces? Who wore these clothes? What conversations were had while wearing them? Who sat on these chairs? What scandals have these objects witnessed, untold? It is the alchemy that vibrates through them that fuels my imagination.

It was 10 years ago that I opened up Coco de Mer. At that time sex shops sold offensive looking objects made out of toxic plastics, in the image of dead body parts. I wanted to create something different. I wanted to seduce and introduce women and men to the doors of their sexual curiosity through beauty and emotions. I wanted to inject love and intimacy into the world of sex. I wanted to express externally what I felt I had locked inside of me.

My yearning desire was to see the visual representation of my own sexuality. By combining my grandmothers cocktail of emotional/sexual lessons with my finely tuned excitement for historical objects, mixed with my spiritual relationship to sex, I creatively gave birth to Coco de Mer. The first luxurious sex shop in the world. I curate Coco de Mer like a museum. Each talent that is under the roof of my exceptional boutique is carefully selected to make sure that desire, peppered with freedom and wrapped in beauty is laced into each and every object.

To me, sex and desire are not things you can prescribe. They are psychological tensions and emotional, spiritual, physical reactions that you can provoke but not package. The truth is, sex and desire hold the magic ingredients of alchemy that are virtually inexplicable. It is the dance, however, to try to put the genie in the bottle that has to be one of the greatest challenges of them all. Like a magpie to a shining trinket, I have seen countless people seduced into exploring their bodies simply because an object was so beautiful. This kind of trickery with the right degree of kindness has released countless unsuspecting customers into a liberation that makes them feel good about themselves, their lovers, and their bodies.

Objects of sexual desire, for me, hold a purpose beyond admiration. They can be a true vehicle for personal happiness and exploration, only, of course, if desire is kept in check and balance.

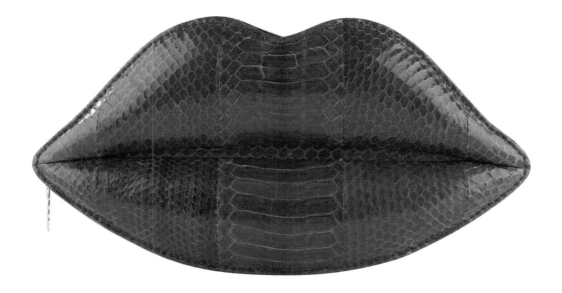

'Vintage Red Lips Snakeskin Clutch' by
Lulu Guinness

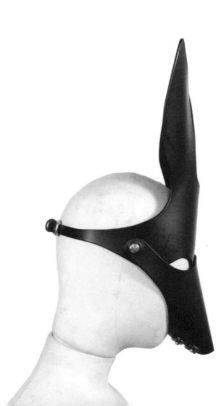

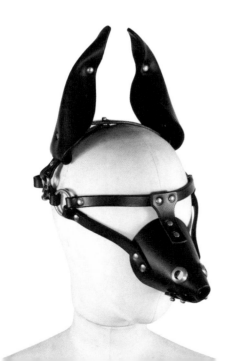

"By believing passionately in something that still does not exist, we create it. The nonexistent is whatever we have not sufficiently desired."
—Franz Kafka

"I have no words only desire" was once written to me, a lover's response to an evocative image, a self-portrait, which I had sent. Simple in its depiction it showed, in close up, only dark hair and a deep pink mouth. No features particularly decipherable yet this image alluded to a state of unkempt tangle and a passion found in the state of merging. With these few words, pure essence within language, desire was full and known. With these few words, and by design, my desire and desires perpetuated and kindled.

Desire.
It comes in many forms and in many levels of intensity and understanding. A heart's desire or longing; that which stems from our innate being or instinct, can be difficult and confusing for the mind to negotiate for the passion resonates on a frequency, which is beyond reason and logic. The mind might labour to fulfil the pull of desire to a finite end rather than simply submitting and surrendering to the flow of the desire as an impulse energy and finding fulfilment in the voyage. We either act upon desire or we suppress it but this transcends the purely physical. Desire is a driving force and another way of seeing. Tied to the imagination and connected to our need for pleasure and satisfaction and for a sense of self worth. Our desires are forever evolving and what we reach for, strive for, enables us to evolve as beings. It is a fundamental and crucial element to our evolution and growth.

It would be foolish to attempt to speak about desire from a purely sexual point of view because if we have no desire we are simply not alive. However, desire is inextricably and intimately connected to Eros and all that resonates with love, passions, wanting and longings. Desire made flesh and all that is sexual, for without doubt, a world devoid of sexual desire would be a world devoid of life. Desire is what drives us to reach out and touch and compels us to connect and join the emotional threads, which bind us. We are all created from the essence of desire and in so many ways it is that which sustains us.

"Man is a creation of desire, not a creation of need."
—Bachelard

Our world is founded upon desire. Desires of the mind and of the body, of the heart and of the spirit. Whether we take the choice to journey toward and meet our desires, or seek a liberation and freedom from them; 'desire' as the motivational force remains

'Bunny Ears', 'Fox Mask' and 'Dog Mask' by Fleet Ilya. Leather

at the core. In taking the conscious decision to be free from the flow of sense-desire, as an act within itself requires, the 'desire' and discipline to find the release from the physical body. The Buddhist monks attempt to 'generate desire' for the purpose and benefit of cultivating what are considered 'skilful qualities' and abandoning those, which are 'unskilful.' Desire as a motivational force, a theme, a concept and a philosophy. Thwarted desire, unrequited desire. Where would we be without desire? Eve would certainly not have picked the apple.

The simple act of saying the word 'desire,' has the capacity to take our imaginings on a journey and to ignite our minds eye, to make it wander and daydream. Consider the emotions felt as you say the word to yourself. Desire. One small word and we are saturated by a vast array of emotions, memories, losses and hopes. The sensations and interpretations are many and infinite. The search to find desire or to consciously deny desire is a unifying experience in as much as it remains a driving force whether embracing, accepting or negating.

Before we journey further into desire we should perhaps consider, or try to imagine, for a moment, the absence of desire. How we would feel without its presence? Not to reach for a goal, or to have a dream, to create, to have an idea or a vision for something beyond ourselves. No desire for connection and intimacy, love and passion, warmth and life. It would be tantamount to imagining a day without light. Living without breath.

Desire is the spark, which is there within all of us and as such it is important that we pay homage to our hearts desire and rhythmic intuition in order to gain new perspectives. Central to this, and in the creation of a personal narrative, is tending to our desire as if it were a garden. Nurture it, nourish it, stimulate the imagination and experience the bloom. And in feeding the imagination we also breathe new life and energy into the physical realm.

Through the pages within the book, desire is explored and demonstrated, not as a separate sexual entity, but in the context of the sensuality of desire and the intensity of emotional experience being part of a greater whole. Certainly the erotic and lustful are depicted and evident but these play alongside delight, wonder, veracity, lyricism, dark romance and beauty. All unified by a particular textural sensibility and then, finally, embellished with a twist of the perverse. The objects, creations, musings and thoughts come from a range of talents with a broad creative mindset who apparently share a wilful regard toward desire in its various manifestations and as an elemental component within their creativity.

The forthcoming curated objects might appear to be either expressions of desire and Eros or incremental to the flourishing of desire. The most stimulating objects and ideas seem to spill into various categories or else cannot be categorised. There is a blatant disregard

'The Steel Heel' by Chau Har Lee.
Steel and leather

for homogeneity and few of the pieces are so implicit that the use or outcome is dictated or formulaic. How we engage with these objects and ideas relates to aspects of our personal journeys and how we make these stories our own, by exploring our erotic and sensuous impulses and how these might be augmented within a framework of love and trust. Many of the pieces seduce with their luscious tactility, displaying hidden or unarticulated desires and providing a link between fantasy and possibility and a nudge toward something other. Bridging the space between our private imaginings and the physical world.

"Imagination is everything. It is the preview of life's coming attractions."
—Albert Einstein

There is a celebratory element to the sexual nature of the book, which is not intended to titillate but rather to reveal and stir sensorially, erotically and joyfully. There is a beautiful reality in the nakedness of many of the objects and an implicit honesty, which is far from sterile.

The book is divided into three distinct phases and the tempo of the book changes and shifts as we travel through the three chapters: Generating, Contemplating and Fulfilling. In Generating desire the sense of touch and physical engagement is not just encouraged, it is emphatically demanded. In Contemplating desire we 'see' desire's textures but we are, predominantly, prohibited or unable to touch. There is such a world of conflict to be lived in desires. Fortunately we ultimately make our way to Fulfilling desire, where it is not just about physical engagement as it is about total immersion. And here you will find housed the Cabinet of Desire, a small well-fingered book, in which nine artists have created a text exploring ideas and thoughts around the subject of desire. Enjoy.

My wishes for this book is that the curated objects combined with the writings, different perspectives, and thoughts, delight and encourage your own private wonderings and wanderings of and through desire and then I hope you go out of your way to put these thoughts into touch.

"Without this playing with fantasy no creative work has ever yet come to birth. The debt we owe to the play of the imagination is incalculable."
—Jung

'Blow Me!' (Warm Collection) by Rebecca
Wilson 2011. Cast porcelain and glass with
gold lustre and found objects

GENERATING
DESIRE

"The imagination is the spur of delights... all depends upon it, it is the mainspring of everything; now, is it not by means of the imagination one knows joy? Is it not of the imagination that the sharpest pleasures arise?"
Marquis de Sade

Surely the best place to generate and engender desire is in the imagination for here it can roam and explore freely. Without inhibition and without constraint it can cavort with the unexpected and play with the bizarre. The imagination has no limits, only those that we impose upon it. But the mind is powerful and the palette vast, for even in the days when we are tired and subdued by the rational limits we have consciously or unconsciously imposed upon ourselves and our lives; in dreamtime the mind overcomes these boundaries of restriction, pays little heed to social mores, and our image journeys become infinite.

So in generating desire, let us trigger the imagination through the sensory experience and explore objects as subjects, which entice us to feel them, to touch them, to smell them and hold them, face to face; soliciting our imaginings with their resonant tactility.

The deliberate object accumulations curated in this section combine the exquisite with the rude, the fetishistic, perverse, the surreal, the sensuous, the lustful and joyful. Unified in their open and covert sexuality. Some pieces tiptoe into the realm of the magical while others thrust their way into the viscera of eroticism. Each in some shape or form tapping into both our conscious and unconscious desires either through material or by design. In some ways they become conduits for our pleasures, insisting upon the feelings of the flesh and inspiring or channeling the lustful utterances and longings of the mind. Fantasies and dreams transpose with the physical world; mingling our most fundamental sense desires with the extraordinary. These objects seem

to spill out of the imagination of their creators and facilitate or encourage us to realize ours.

Many of the pieces chosen to generate desire share an obsessive like attention to detail in the process of their creation or in their textural vision. The substance of these objects is particular. Raw, natural and unexpected materials are worked with exquisite craftsmanship, tempting the senses with their erotic charm. Beautiful fusions between mind and body, the named and the abstract; straddling language and narrative, fashion and art, ornamentation and product design in an unrestrictive in-between or poly-space where thoughts, wonderings and ideas meet, flow and dance with Eros.

As children we are encouraged to look but we must not touch. Our fundamental need and desire to make real our physical world is inhibited. But in holding, through holding, stroking, fingering, caressing.....being with, we come to know, recognize and understand not only our physical selves but our place and connection to and within a greater whole. Our sensorial knowledge, the feelings of the flesh, serve as signs or markers for our physical and emotional well-being. Through the appreciation of our senses and sensuality we are able to take pride, power, control and pleasure in our own sexuality.

Our deepest emotions are almost entirely connected to profound memory and vivid sensory experience. The remarkable smell, feel, taste, sound and form of something might act as a lightening rod, a lens of focus that allow us memorable purchase and egress and a return, to a moment of elevated consciousness within a fashioned garden and playground. These things, these objects, these belongings of the imagination mingle and marry fantastic thought with the visceral and concrete, bridging the virtual and the real, desire and being, dreaming and living.

In Generating desire we pay homage to the senses and journey through five phases of texture, tempo and pulse. Beginning, gently at first, by stroking the skin and exploring silks, lace, scents and flowers; the fabrics which romance and caress.

Then distracted by a glinting, the magpie fetish is momentarily caught; jewels, pearls, silver and gold, objects that glitter and sparkle attract and play to the eye. But delighting in senses of touch, the flesh returns to resume affectionate pleasure-seeking with strokes and tickles of feathers, fur and locks of hair.

With an increased pulse, rhythm and resolve; latex and leather hold firmly and tight. Held and contained within the structure of a corset and restricted with particular precision and beauty in rope.

All these objects and images feed the imagination and tantalize the intimate senses, those that intoxicate with proximity. The closer one comes to the source of these desires the more one opens.

In desire beats the heart and we enter openly into the 'O's.

Let Us Begin Gently
by Tracing the Skin:

"A PETTICOAT
A light white, a disgrace, an ink spot, a rosy charm."
— Gertrude Stein

After the mind, and heart, our skin is the largest erogenous zone and it covers us entirely. It is our shield, veil and Achilles heel, the protective and responsive layer between our interior selves and the exterior world. On meeting the sensations of cold, heat, pressure and vibration, the varied nerve endings attentively reply.

Lace awakens a curiosity for it is the revealing absence and nakedness within the fabric that makes it so desirable. The skin is exposed beneath the openings of the weave, creating a flirtatious balance between that which is revealed, and that which is concealed.

Similarly with the nylon of a stocking: the transparency of the fine gauze lies on top of the skin and highlights the skin's texture, drawing a defined outline around the shape of the leg. The flesh is covered yet it is unable to hide. Skin within skin, contained and defined as natural and naked.

Silks conceal to varying degrees depending upon the density of the weave. Gossamer light chiffons through to smooth and weighty lustrous satins,

mask and screen the tone and texture of the skin. But in this covering the body's form and contours are exposed. The pure fabric breathes and sighs and slides with the skin's nuances, becoming warm when the skin is cool and cool when the skin becomes warm.

Flowers, perfumes and scents are so inextricably linked and connected with the romance of desire; of loves found and lovers spellbound. Flowers rich with symbolism and scent delight and gratify the olfactory senses. For it is a primal or innate form of intelligence and understanding and moves instantaneously to heightened feeling, emotion and memory. Permeating the boundary of exteriority, we breathe in, and move directly into interiority. A wonderful perfume licks and smudges the skin and we meet and merge with it as one.

"If only there could be an invention that bottled up a memory, like scent. And it never faded, and it never got stale. And then, when one wanted it, the bottle could be uncorked, and it would be like living the moment all over again."
— Daphne du Maurier, Rebecca

'Butterfly Torso' by Paul Seville and Steph Aman. Leather and silk

Opposite page: 'Widows of Culloden'
dress by Alexander McQueen. A/W
2006–7. Cream silk tulle and lace with
resin antlers

'Flora' Orchid 02 by Alidra Alić. Silver

'Camisole' and 'Bloomers' by Stephanie
Loungewear. Silk chiffon and tulle

Opposite page: 'Baby Doll with
'soutache' motifs by Jean Paul Gaultier.
La Perla Designer Collection F/W
2010. Silk chiffon

**'UNDERWEAR NO. 2' FROM THE SERIES 'UNDERWEAR FOR MEN' 2007
BY ALISTER MACKIE**

"The idea was instigated by Nick Knight, who wanted to shoot women's inspired underwear for men. So I developed a series of undergarments that used and incorporated vintage corsetry and materials. Each piece was fitted to accommodate a man's body and shape but was created with the intention of being as erotic and sensuous as women's lingerie. We subverted the lines between masculine and feminine. I also wanted the guy who was wearing the underwear to be desirable, but the pieces in themselves to be desirable as objects. We recently framed the series of six pieces for an exhibition at SHOWstudio and they look quite beautiful behind glass. They have become erotic artefacts."

'Underwear No.2' from the series
'Underwear for Men' by Alister Mackie
2007. Mixed media. 43cm x 46 cm x 2cm

Opposite page: 'Flora' Orchid 03 by
Alidra Alić. Plastic

'Alice's Adventures in Wonderland'
Drink Me by Alidra Alić Freshwater
pearls and plastic

'Sans Jupons 2 Tulle Nude'
by N De Samin. Silk

'Tangled Necklace' by Julia deVille. Sterling silver and human hair

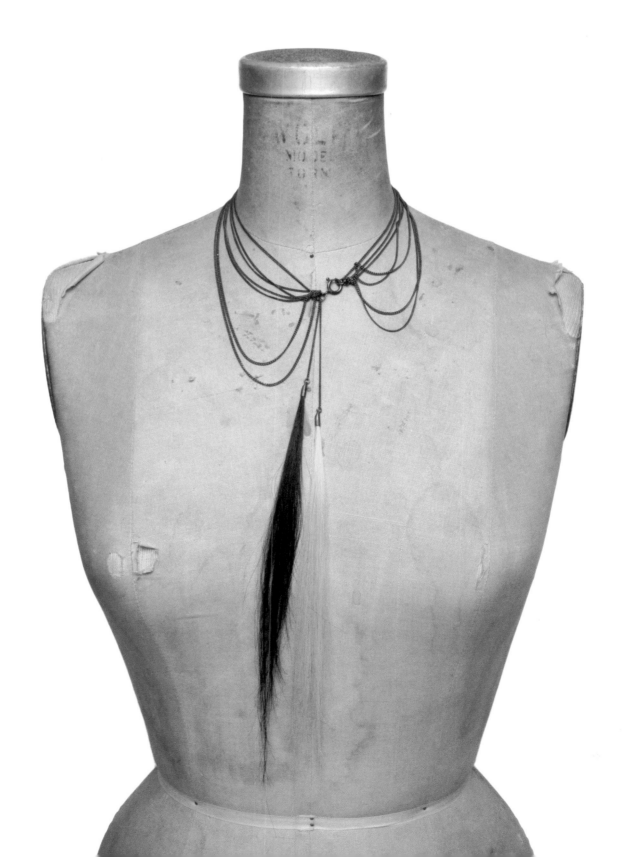

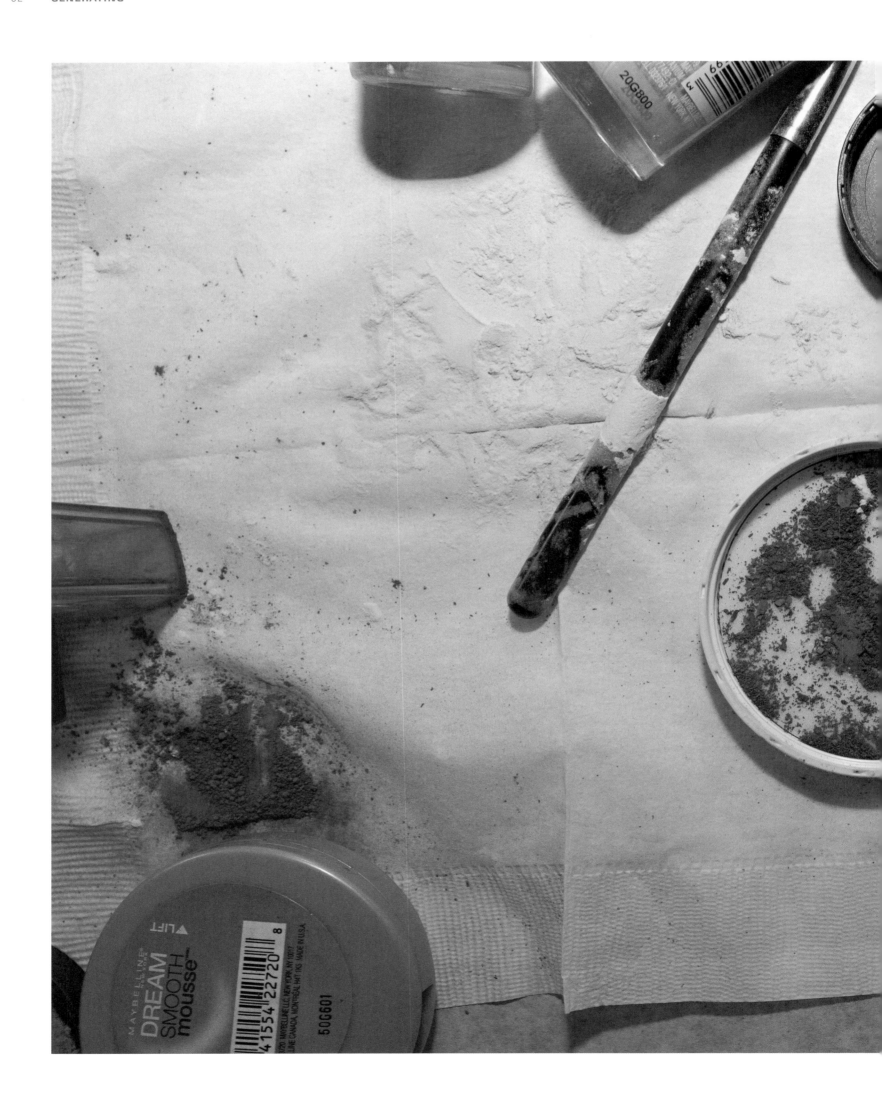

Opposite page: 'Geisha' by Kunza
Corsetiere and Adam Lach. Antique silk
kimonos and silk corset

'Flora' Hyacinth 01 by Alidra Alić .
Silver, plastic and strawberry quartz

Opposite page: 'Sarabande' dress by
Alexander McQueen. S/S 2007. Nude
silk organza embroidered with silk
flowers and fresh flowers

'The Stink Bombs' by Cire Trudon.
Glass bombs to throw onto the ground;
rising and filling the surrounding area
with an explosion of perfume

Composite 0901 by Fileti © 2011.
'A Private Function' by Strumpet & Pink

Opposite page: 'Vinatge Parachute
Couture Dress and Hood' by
Rachel Freire

'Couture Ecco Leather Jacket'
by Rachel Freire. S/S 2011

'Lipstick Rose' by Ralf Schwieger for Editions de Parfums Frédéric Malle.

"This scent is as merry as a dash of lipstick with its rose and violet flavored scent. A vision of glamorized femininity, the saucy lady doing her make-up in a mirror"

'Hunting Through the Ruffles (exploded and capped)' by Strumpet & Pink. Silk chiffon

The Lake & Stars F/W 2010 Campaign

Pandering to the Magpie Fetish:

"There's a lady who's sure all that glitters is gold, and she's buying a stairway to heaven."
–Led Zeppelin

All that glitters, all that sparkles in our eyes; our gaze is unconsciously drawn, for the light and reflections dance in our careful watch. Flickering, glinting, catching the light, never still, reflecting and mirroring, infinite and minute aspects of ourselves and what lies beyond. We are drawn to the shimmering sun dancing ripples on the water and to the twinkle of the stars in the dark of night. For it is here that our thoughts and wonderings tangibly grasp a universal desire, one that reaches far beyond ourselves.

Desire. From the Latin "de-sidus" to turn our eyes from the stars or translated literally as *'to stop contemplating the stars for religious meanings'*. Desire dances where our wonderings linger.

It is of little wonder therefore that a jewel, a glinting, intricate image of beauty, artistry, lustre and setting, holds an allure and seduces our visual focus. We covet shining objects of desire and jewelry not only for their visual de-light, but as meaningful symbols and forms of personal and social expression. Jewels and jewellery have forever been worn to adorn the

body, as amulets and talismans and given as tokens and demonstrations of love. They retain our emotions, resound ancestry and bond us to our memories. Every gemstone resonates and we connect with them on many levels as they carry and transfer mystical powers to the wearer. We know the feeling of absence when a particular ring is not worn on a finger. The discomfort of a missing in balance or symmetry is physically present as absence felt.

Jewelry has always functioned as a form of currency but it has shifted and evolved over time, demonstrating wealth and social status, display and ornamentation to fashion accessory and as an item of artistic expression. Similarly the purpose of jewelry has changed through the ages from being a practical and viable object such as a buckle, pin or brooch, designed to hold a fabric in place, to becoming an object of desire to embellish and enhance personal presentation and beauty. The color and shine or lustre and sparkle of a gemstone or valuable metal is now prized more than the enchanting magical powers it may possess.

Diamond   *love and the eternity of love*
Emerald   *faithfulness, harmony, good-luck and*
         well being
Ruby   *passion, unbridled love, wisdom, warmth*
         and vitality
Sapphire   *the gem of the heavens; virtue, sincerity,*
         sympathy, harmony, faithfulness and
         indestructible trust
Pearl   *purity*

Amethyst   *forgiveness, trust, piety, sobering and*
         cleansing, protects against seduction
         and believed to encourage celibacy

And what of the pure and deceptive pearl? An iridescent beauty created by chance, from an irritation, a secretion, within the oyster. It is thought that natural pearls form under a set of accidental conditions when a microscopic intruder or parasite enters and settles inside the shell. The mollusk, being irritated by the intruder, forms a pearl sac of external mantle tissue cells and secretes the calcium carbonate and conchiolin to cover the irritant. This secretion process is repeated many times, thus producing a pearl. This annoyance inspires the purest symbol of desire. A pearl earring, and a pearl necklace and how it's once chaste innocence have been transformed with a duplicitous charge.

'Crystal Rose' by Noritaka Tatehana. Chimera Spring Summer 2011.
Red Swarovski and gold-studded sole

'The String of Pearls Massage Ring'
by Betony Vernon. Cultured pearls and
sterling silver. *"The sensuous powers
would never be suspected but those
who are 'in the know' prize it for bringing a new and luxurious dimension to
intimate massage"*

Opposite page: Pearl Restraints'
by Kiki de Montparnasse. 10 feet of
harvested pearls

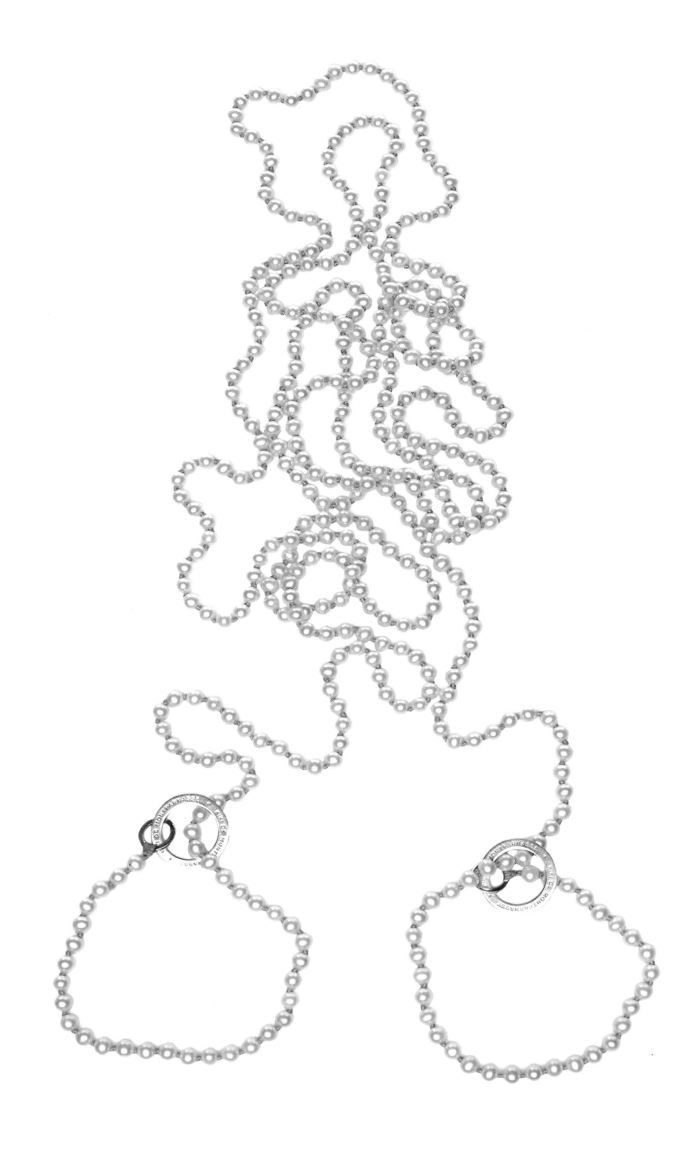

Opposite page: 'Gold Leaf Shakti
Mirror' by Mark Brazier-Jones.
*"A symbol of the female principal,
the gateway through which we enter
this dimension"*

'Divorce Ring' by Gisèle Ganne.
18ct gold-plated electroformed bird
skull and acrylic roses

Opposite page: 'Rhinestone
Embellished Neck Corset in Linen'
by Schipper/Arques

'Lampshade Skirt' by Mary Katrantzou.
S/S 2011

'Lampshade Skirt' by Mary Katrantzou.
S/S 2011

Opposite page: 'Pom-pom Bracelet' by
Miu Miu. Leather and marabou feather

'Emerald City Ring' by Julia deVille.
18ct white gold and emeralds.

"An amalgamation of three different engagement rings. 'Emerald City Ring' is about having many loves although not necessarily in a romantic way. It is about having an open heart and loving all"

'Hotlips Ruby Ring' by Solange
Azagury-Partridge. 18ct blackened
white gold and rubies

Opposite page: 'Ballcrusher Ring' by
Solange Azagury-Partridge. 18ct white
gold, pearl and enamel nails

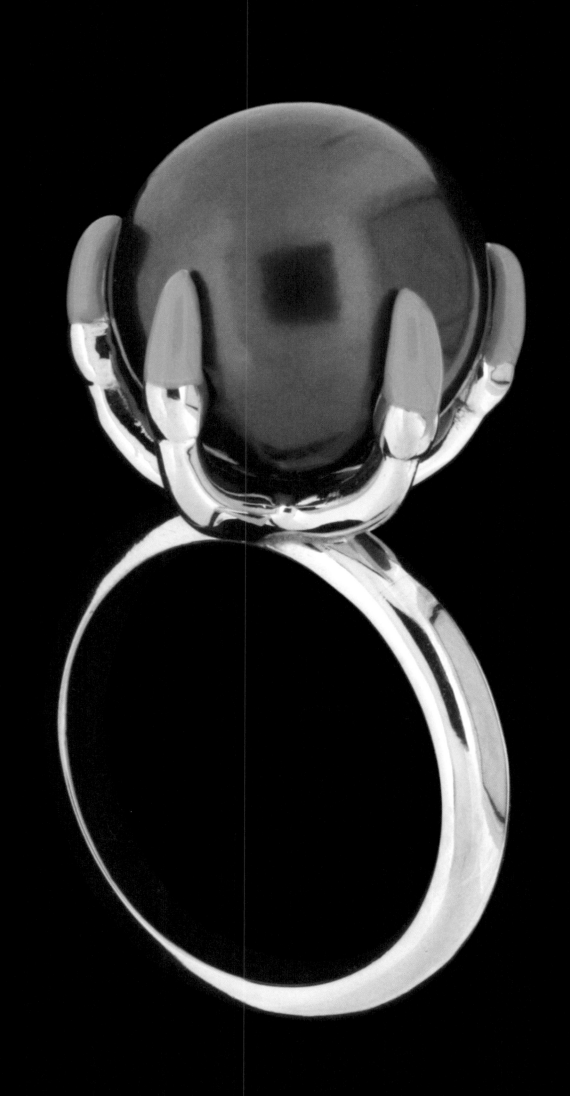

'Poison Bottle' by Golden Chix.
Glass, plastic, brass

Opposite page: 'Hand Embroidered
Mask' by Coco de Mer. Velvet

'Sex on the Brain' by Piers Atkinson.
S/S 2010. Cherry ball gag and
heavy-duty leather

GENERATING DESIRE

"Then stay with me a little longer,' Madame Olenska said in a low tone, just touching his knee with her plumed fan. It was the lightest touch, but it thrilled him like a caress. "
–Edith Wharton. The Age of Innocence

The opulent and sumptuous plumes and furs from other animals have always held an attraction, force and fascination. A feathers connection to the colourful and exotic, to ceremony and to elaborate mating rituals has, no doubt, been incremental in their seductive and flirtatious appeal. A wonder found in the remarkable combination of an intricate and elaborate beauty, incredible strength, energy and a barely there light-ness. In adornment feathers bring a sense of the striking and the unusual but it is in their marriage with the skies and their link to freedom, flight and transcendence, that delight is felt and made present, as anybody who picks one up will know. And they also tickle. The entire body, as a whole, can be softly tantalised and sensorially stirred with the delicate stroke and caress of a plume.

"Sex pleasure in women is a kind of magic spell; it demands complete abandon; if words or movements oppose the magic of caresses, the spell is broken."
–Simone de Beauvoir

Cherished locks of lovers given and exchanged as keepsakes retain fetish like appeal. In holding the hair from the head of a loved one, a memory and mood is possessed and held close. The human hair fetishization was taken to exquisite heights by the Victorians who would braid hair into jewelry or meticulously weave small locks of hair into fine images to treasure in lockets, worn and held close to the heart. Or a woman might delicately intertwine her own hair with that of her beloved. In *momento mori* intricate memorial creations were woven into symbolic images of loss and mourning as an indication or demonstration that love and desire transcend death.

The hair from the horse is connected to stamina, strength, power and nobility also freedom, energy and the wild. To use such a material is loaded with metaphor and meaning and the wearer of such a material becomes imbued or assumes and connects to the forces and spirit of the beast.

A/W 11 by Phoebe English. Fringed rubber and acrylic hair

Opposite page: 'Sans Jupons 1'
by N De Samin. Silk

'Umbrella' and 'Briefcase' by
Oliver Ruuger. Ebony, leather, brass
and horsehair and mechanical hair

'Bird of Prey' by Gisèle Ganne. Fox tails with 18ct gold-plated sterling silver

The 'Hunting Man' collection by Gisèle Ganne brings together traditional customs and practices that surround the act of hunting, making use of symbols such as the stag, the trophy and the prey. Just as one would display trophies of their hunt, her jewelry invites the wearer to bear the mark of the hunter, symbolizing both the pursuit for a new lover as well as the evidence of conquests.

'D6A Victoria Dress' by Felder Felder
A/W 2011–12. Wool and hand dyed
goat hair

'Ostrich Pleasure Puff Ring' by Betony
Vernon. Ostrich feather and sterling silver

'HOW TO WEAR A FAMOUS PAINTER'

A collection created with paintbrushes, or the alternative of diamonds!
Many of these brushes were the magic sticks of the imagination and created some of
the most beautiful masterpieces in painting. After their life of hard work, they were cast
aside instead of being cherished and made into brilliants.
Do they not posses the same value as diamonds?
—Emanuela Deyanova of Ramjuly

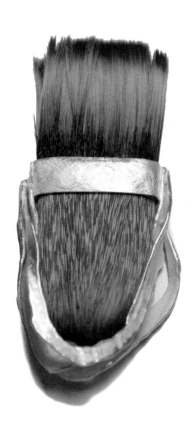

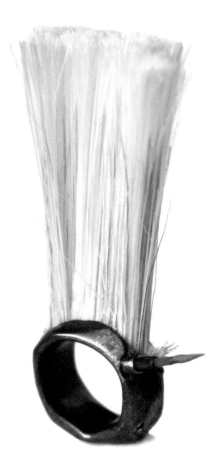

'Koala Diamond Brush' by Ramjuly
2010. Koala bear hair, aluminium, silver
and 24ct gold

'Shaving (High White Brush)'
by Ramjuly 2010. Synthetic hair,
aluminium and silver

Opposite page: 'Sado Chic Collier with Ostrich Feather Tickler' by Betony Vernon. Sterling silver and ostrich feathers

'Feathers Healer Ring' by Betony Vernon. Sterling silver with guinea fowl feathers

INTERVIEW WITH IMMODESTY BLAIZE

WHY ARE FEATHERS SO CONNECTED TO DESIRE AND THE SENSUOUS? Feathers are desired and often fetishized because they have connotations of the exotic; of display, grandeur, and flirtation, of tribal associations, or beauty and freedom. Since they belong to birds, for humans to wear them can be seen as perverse, decadent, even lustful, self indulgent or vulgar. And whilst I believe sensuality is personal to the individual, feathers are sensual to me because they are living, moving, breathing. I love the way the fronds float or flutter on a breeze, and the delicate touch of feather upon skin. Visually they are striking, from the majesty of a spray of hand-dyed pheasant feather to the soft fuzziness of goose down. To wear them in volume there's a sense of luxury and opulence, and they trap your body heat. You have to take care of them and preen them – steam them and fluff them up, or style them and hand tie and curl each frond…they need love.

WHAT ASPECTS DO THEY BRING TO YOUR WORK AND CREATIVITY AS A BURLESQUE ARTIST? There is such variety of texture in feathers; ostrich, swan, pheasant and so on. They are so versatile - they give volume, drama and splendor to a costume, or they can add a softness and femininity. The way they move when dancing adds to the impact of every body movement. When used within the showgirl context they also carry their inherent symbolism of extravagance and display, of coquettishness and the notion of an other-worldly fantasy being…and of course, they are often seen as campy too!

WHAT IS YOUR FAVOURITE FEATHER ACCESSORY OR GARMENT? A three-foot high headdress made for me by renowned milliner Stephen Jones OBE. With a classic satin tri-corn hat as the base, each 48ply ostrich boa extends up, then cascades down my back. These are then taken out mid-performance to become a fan. Stephen intended the headdress to be like a 'striptease' hat that came apart in this way. The piece is very heavy with the weight and drag from the feathers so was constructed with a complex interior wire frame to make it secure on my head while dancing. It took five fittings to create, the wire frame was made in Paris, the feathers hand-dyed and flown in from Vegas. When they say 'light as a feather' it's a complete fallacy, feathers are very heavy! But the effect is beautiful.

WHAT IS YOUR FAVOURITE TYPE OF FEATHER AND WHY? Either egret or swan down. Egret is the most delicate spray, showgirl headdresses and 'backpacks' were often covered in it, and it was the height of splendor and expense in a costume. Herons had evolved their plumage as a way to attract their mates –and it seems they had such a similar effect on humans that sources began to disappear in late 19th century, with herons on the point of extinction. Therefore they should only be seen on the birds or in vintage showgirl photographs. So for me to use today, my favorite feather is goosedown or swandown, as used in a powder puff – impossibly fluffy and sensual. It inspired my original signature powder puff act, with which I won the Burlesque Hall of Fame crown in Las Vegas.

Opposite page: Image courtesy of
Immodesty Blaize

'Unfaithful Feather Duster' by Nika
Zupanc. Ostrich feather and lacquer

Opposite page: A/W 2011 by Charlie le
Mindu. Human hair, pvc and lace

'Hand Embroidered Mask' by Coco de
Mer. Silk

'Paris' by Piers Atkinson. A/W 2011. *"A nod to 1930's Paris – it's heyday of tete-a-tetes in seedy back alleys,* *lovers on park benches at dusk, drag queens in late night cabarets..."* 'Isabella' and 'Flesh Choker' by Piers Atkinson. It is later than you think A/W 2010

Top: 'One Day I Looked into the Deep Blue Sky' 2011. Turned phenolic acid plastic, rhodium plated silver, human hair. 250mm x 150mm. (not including hair)

Bottom: 'Beauty is a Modern Domain' 2011. Rhodium plated silver, phenolic acid plastic, walnut, leather, fabric. 500 mm x 250mm x 190mm

Top: 'Noli me tangere' 2009. Rhodium plated silver, leather, human hair. 180mm x 65mm (not including hair)

Bottom: 'The Voyeurism of Violence & Villainy' 2011. Turned phenolic acid plastic, oxidised silver, fabric. 570mm x 200mm

All pieces by Mark Woods

'Tulle corset with feathers' by La Perla
Black Label. S/S 2008

Opposite page: 'Daphne' neckpiece by   'YVA' by Lelo. 18ct gold plate
Maryam Keyhani. A/W 2011. Lambskin
and rooster feather

O'ha bracelet' by Derrick R. Cruz of
Black Sheep & Prodigal Sons.
Horse hair.

"My father 'Jun' an adoptee of a Navajo
tribe, taught me about the transfer of
spirit and power from animal to human.
That for every sacrifice there should be
respect offered as recompense. From
this exchange a greater being emerges
as we become one with the sacrificed."

98 **Hold Me Firmly,
Hold Me Tight:**

*"And the day came when the risk to remain tight
in a bud was more painful than the risk it took
to blossom."*
– Anaïs Nin

Hold Me Firmly, Hold Me Tight; a confine within
limits. The need and urge to be held is connected to
our time within the womb. In this restricted space
our movement is limited, we are secured, fastened,
protected and safe. Our innate desire and need to
be held and embraced does not diminish but its
meaning may shift. In restraint, movement is narrowed; in limiting the perimeters of our physical
command we are compelled to release and relinquish our emotional control. Placing ourselves into
the hands of another requires understanding and a
considerable level of trust for in our disarmed help-
less-ness, we are obliged to accept our pleasure.

A corset firmly holds the body and provides physical
support. It straightens the back and improves pos-
ture. But is also narrows the waist and within firm
fabric borders, accentuates and exaggerates the
full-ness of curves. For some the experience is
supportively binding while for others it is constric-
tively narrowing.

Leather can hold very firmly and may hold very tight.
In wearing leather, being held by and within leather,
we take on some of the attributes of the initial
creature's Chi and power. There is the frisson in
touching something similar to our own naked-ness
and yet it is distinct and separate. Yet, however it
is treated and sanitized we are unable to ignore the
marks and origins of a life; the irregularities found
in blemishes, wrinkles and small scratches are present and make themselves known. Time and again,
a skin within skin is adorned in form and figure. This
firm outer-muscle becomes an empowered sexual
affirmation as the wearer breathes new life into the
garment worn.

The properties of leather make it malleable and
responsive and in molding to the shape of the body,
through use and wear, it becomes individually per-
sonalized. While ritualistic garments such as animal
like headdresses feed into the materials theatricality,
a liberation is found and discovered in the wearing
of masks. An animal like identity is projected and we
are freed to play a part.

Latex is skin-tight and becomes a shiny second-skin.
It requires dexterity to get into and determination

in facilitating its removal. Visually it is seamless and
although entirely covered, the wearer appears as
naked and the body disclosed. In this way shape
and form is enhanced and the silhouette redefined
in a similar vein to the corset but without the defined structure. Latex firmly holds and squeezes
yet is smooth to the touch and warms with the
temperature of the body. The very fact that this
rubber skin prohibits the under-skin from breathing
further enhances the drama of wearing. One skin
wears another, enclosed and hermetic, revealed and
smothered, sealed and revealed.

In creative hands, rope can be artistically employed
to construct a full body hug; a tight embrace from
head to toe. Adeptly tied and applied, critical pressure and pleasure points on the body are caressed,
pressed and embraced in the process of fashioning
a visually desirable wrapping. Without the sense
of movement we are bound, we are supported and
held by intricate and decorative patterns in rope. The
binding and tying enhances the focus on the pleasure aesthetics of the erotic. The lines of bondage
connect us to the other(s) in a performance of stric-
ture and surrender. We are literally and figuratively
suspended, cradled, and set free.

'Joy Dress' and 'Blinkers' by Atsuko Kudo. Latex

'Cushion and Gag Set' by Fleet Ilya.
Leather

Opposite page: 'Gold Buckle Cuff'
by Maison Martin Margiela. Brass

'Cuff' by Bliss Lau. Lambskin, liquid
hematite plated brass

Kunza Corsetiere limited edition
signature silk cinchers, decorated with
authentic English Victorian jet appli-
qués and antique French chantilly lace

'Antique Lace Leather Gauntlets'
by Paul Seville. Leather

Opposite page: 'Sans Culottes'
by N De Samin

ATSUKO KUDO – LATEX QUESTION

Japanese born, London-based designer Atsuko Kudo has been producing exquisitely feminine designs exclusively in latex since 2001. She is feted for her pioneering techniques with latex fabric and combines her exclusive prints with filigree and folding techniques, which create her unique and instantly recognizable style. It is the surprising and striking fusion between a fabric that, until Atsuko, has previously been rooted in fetish wear, and her couture approach, which can be said to define her style.

WHAT IS IT THAT MAKES LATEX SO DESIRABLE? Atsuko Kudo: "Latex empowers women. When you wear latex you feel special – like a super woman. Latex is like a shiny second skin, very nice to touch. When it's cut well and used in the correct gauge, latex gives magic to a woman's body. It's like the ultimate shape wear that anyone can have. I want latex to create a positive, sensual feeling so I am always trying to create that when I design and produce the clothes. It's not about a dark feeling - for me it's uplifting and a celebration of love."

"My desire is to make the world a more beautiful, shiny and sexy place."

'Cage Chandelier' by Fleet Ilya. Leather   Opposite page: 'Chastity Corset'
with padlock closure and 'Museliere
(muzzle) Mask' by Schipper/Arques

FLEET ILYA — DESIRE QUESTIONS

Fleet Ilya can be traced back to a small bedroom in South London where Russian-born Ilya Fleet began combining his training in traditional saddle making with a knowledge of three-dimensional design which he learned from his late father, a renowned Russian sculptor. The constructive tendencies are evident in his rigorous pursuit of functionality and a sublimity of form.

Ilya soon developed what is widely regarded as the signature line 'Restraint'; a collection of handcrafted luxury accessories for the sexually playful. Resha Sharma became his creative partner and wife shortly afterwards. In applying her knowledge of fashion, image making and art direction, Fleet Ilya has developed a design ethos without boundaries, producing dynamic work across fashion, bondage and interiors and blurring the line between leather bondage and personal adornment.

Do you remember the first object or artefact that you saw and desired?
RESHA: It was a pair of T-bar, plum, patent shoes, I was about four years old.
How would you define desire?
RESHA: A want that turns into a need.
Does desire for you come from the inside out or the outside in?
RESHA: Inside out
Your works are fully formed objects of desire in themselves. Is this compounded because they enhance desire or is this due to the artisan craftsmanship and the luxurious materials that you use?
ILYA: A combination of the two; the desirability of our pieces as objects are of equal importance to the desire they create when worn.
Within your designs do you feel there are certain qualities or materials that make your work more desirable?
ILYA: Well, our primary material, leather, has a great appeal for many even before it takes on a form. The standard of the execution of our ideas using the leather is where we aim to create further desire, every 'Restraint' piece is handmade in our studio. I think something that is handmade has a certain energy present.
Do you believe that a mass-produced item could become an object of desire?
ILYA: Yes as there are many levels of desire, but it depends on the person, for some it is more desirable to obtain something very few have.
When you are developing a new piece are you making manifest an experience, an emotion, or do you, quite simply, see the idea, a piece, as fully formed?

ILYA: Some pieces have more emotional attachment than others, but many are born from a desire either of my own or someone I know. The most successful pieces have been created in this way.
What material/s do you find most desirable and why?
RESHA: There are many, obviously I have a thing for leather, it's a super sexy material, it lends itself very well to manipulation.
Do you feel there is a difference in the way a woman desires or manifests desire and the way a man desires or manifests desire?
RESHA: At the core of it; no; I think it can be all consuming for both sexes.
We seem to be living in a time whereby everything is 'sexy'. We are surrounded by a visual sexiness and yet there seems to be a real separation between that which is sexy and that which is sex and/or sexual. There is a two-dimensional quality about the 'sexy' we are surrounded by that only speaks of surface. There seems to be little understanding of sexuality and the true depth and breadth of it. What makes it three-dimensional?
ILYA: Truth
What was the first piece that you created and what inspired or provoked you to create such a piece?
ILYA: The first ever piece was a cuff, which was made specifically for clubbing. It had two compartments, one for cigarettes and the other for my lighter. The first bondage piece was a harness with cuff attachments on the back for my girlfriend at the time.

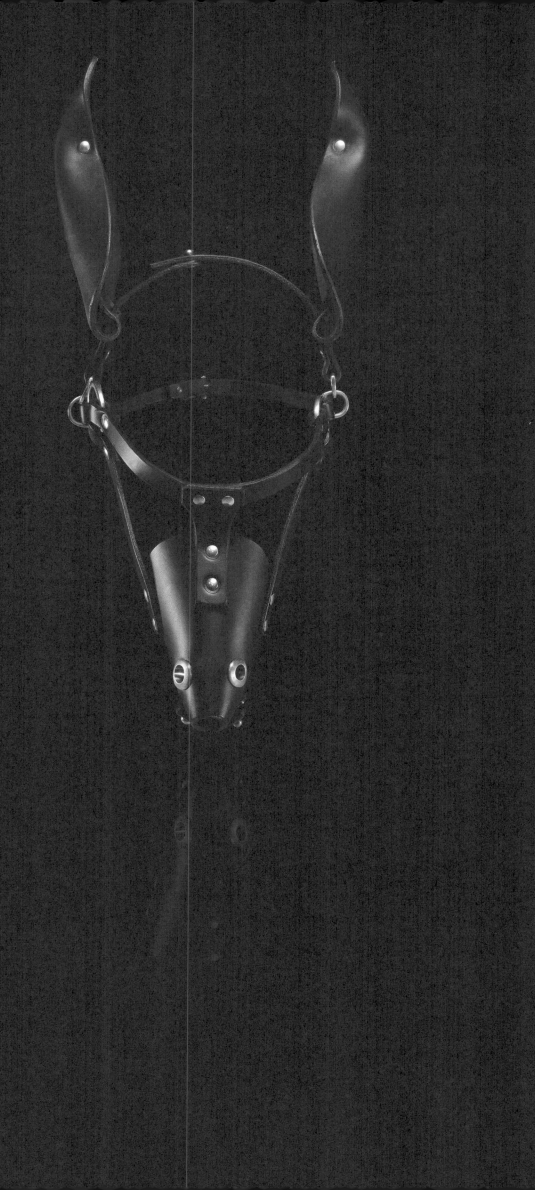

'Dog Mask' by Fleet Ilya. Leather

'Corset Harness' by Fleet Ilya, SS11.
Leather

Opposite page: 'Racer Back Harness'
and 'Cut Out Belt' by Fleet Ilya.
Leather

'Web Body Piece' by Fleet Ilya. Leather

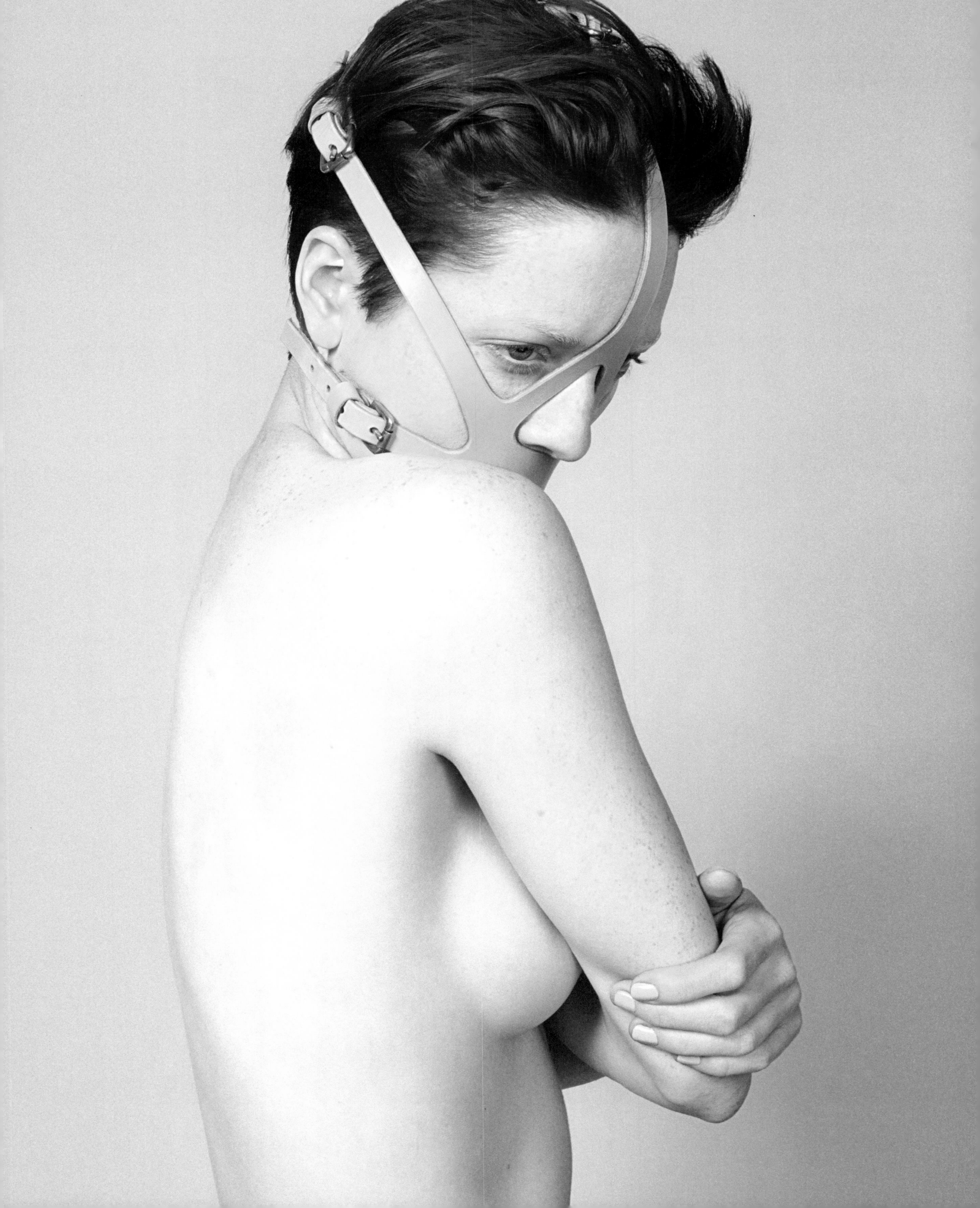

Cage Mask' by Fleet Ilya. Leather

'Dawn Ritual' by Aoi Kotsuhiroi. 2011. Urushi lacquered horns (heels), Urushi lacquered cherry tree, leather.

"These feet objects are exclusively 'restricted' for the 'walks' through the bedroom.... As in Kinbaku Art, the leather straps can be tied up around the feet and the objects in different manners to reveal the beauty."

SHIBARI BY MIDORI

Until recently Shibari, or Japanese rope bondage, with its intricate patterns binding bodies alluringly, was the rarefied pleasure of the red-light districts in Japan and its niche market pornography. Beyond the shores of the Land of the Rising Sun, only scattered pockets of quiet enthusiasts indulged in this form of rope play. Even in early 90's, as I began to explore this pleasure more deeply, lovers who had heard of Shibari were rare and teachers were even scarcer.

Things have changed considerably today. Now it's a titillating open secret for the sexually adventurous. Practitioners are numerous, the net buzzes incessantly about it, rope conventions and parties flourish all over, and it pops up unexpectedly in television segments. (My favorite example of the latter was a passing reference made nonchalantly on a travel food show by an infamous chef.) It's draw and soaring popularity isn't surprising. We are always seeking 'the next great thing' of sex, pleasure and intimacy. Shibari's Japanese provenance alone allures many. We do so love the mysteries of the Orient, whether real or fabricated. Flamed by the power of the web, Japanese bondage imagery has reached a wide audience. Simultaneously the web has also fueled a quasi-historical digital folklore of Shibari's origins, cultural legitimacy and supposed spirituality in Japan. Again, we do so love the mysteries of the Orient. (It is ironic, however, that most rope practitioners in Japan have no clue at all of the fanatical devotional interest in Shibari exploding in the West.)

Far from being an esoteric tradition, descended from the ways of the warriors and mountain monks, it's developed into its erotic form in the ripe womb of sex work and commercial entertainment. Even today, from a few inquiries with the right person you'll soon find yourself in a small establishment deep in the red light district watching a comely lass bound and displayed like some carnal flower arrangement. The ropes fly from the hands of the dominant as fast as swords fly in a Kurosawa movie. The patrons sit back, drinks in hand, and watch the tableaux unfold, night after night. This reality has sadly been sanitized out from the narrative reverentially repeated in the West. I suspect this has more to do with the deep discomfort Westerners have with commercialized erotic entertainment. Which is a terrible shame, actually, as the red-light districts of Japan can be a ton of naughty fun.

What's often unappreciated is the Japanese obsession with wrapping, packaging and design. For a culture that so deeply obsesses over design from textile, clothing, architecture, to food, it's only natural that their sexual imagery should be so finely wrapped with repetitive patterns pleasing to the eyes and thrilling on the skin. Whether motivated by a pure desire for new pleasures, by a wish to delight one's partner, or by cloying Orientalism, the practitioner soon falls into the rabbit hole of Shibari's pleasures.

At a fundamental level they discover the potential for creativity, connection, intimacy and savoring a protracted erotic encounter. You can't just kiss, sex and go to sleep. It's not just slapping handcuffs on an outstretched limb. Even the fastest roper must take the time needed to tie and come to the play with intentionality and a plan. Part of the attraction may be in its slow and organic nature. It's a pleasure form that requires education, practice and ongoing acquisition of skill to hone an expertise – an antithesis of this era of immediacy and instant gratification. One must take the time to become proficient. Hard earned mastery and expertise is fetishized more than ever today.

The ropes themselves are ancient materials of cotton or hemp, a tactile and subconscious reminder of our agrarian ancestry pre-Industrial humanity. It's delightfully, simply analog in the digital age. Shibari requires process in planning, weaving and unwrapping. It's sexuality's backlash against the ready-made pre-fab life – it's own Slow Movement, not unlike the Slow Food Movement. As the ropes are brought out and the encounter is plotted, there is sweet anticipation. As the lover is woven in there is pleasure. As skin is played with, there is pleasure (and perhaps a few orgasms). Even as the ropes are removed there is pleasure. As the lover caresses the rope over willing flesh, the attention is lavished on the whole person. With Japanese style rope the body can no longer be reduced to the simple shagging components of mouth, nipples, breasts, cock, pussy and butt. The whole body, whole person and all the every bit of delicious skin surface become the playground of sensation. For some lovers, this is just the cure for a lack luster and predictable sex life.

Above all, rope demands creativity and sense of visual aesthetics. Certain patterns repeat from the smallest details to the largest areas. Squares, diamonds, hexagon. The one tying must determine the placement of the ropes, the body position, what ties to where, level of tension, emotional and sensual impact on the bound lover. The form must tickle the fancy of all parties involved. Beyond the erotic functionality it must play to the lover's gaze to savor the contours, musculature and exposure. The twist of a body or limb alone may shift the visual and direct experience from mundane to mind-blowing.

Shibari creates erotic delight for the lovers by romantically harking back to an imagined past, awakening the skin, challenging the creative mind, feeding the beauty craving heart, stoking the flames of lust and entwining hearts to one another.

'Shelves' by Midori © 2005
Photo and rope art

Opposite page: 'Skeleton Corset Belt',   'Horse Tail Corset Belt' by Paul Seville.
'Ostrich Spanking Paddle' and 'Ebony   Leather and horsehair. 'Embroidered
Stingray Corsage' by Paul Seville. Leather   Chemise' by Stephanie Loungewear. Silk

Opposite page: 'Pilgrim Hooves' by
Gabriella Marina Gonzalez. Leather

'Bodice' and 'Arm Cuff' by Gabriella
Marina Gonzalez. Leather

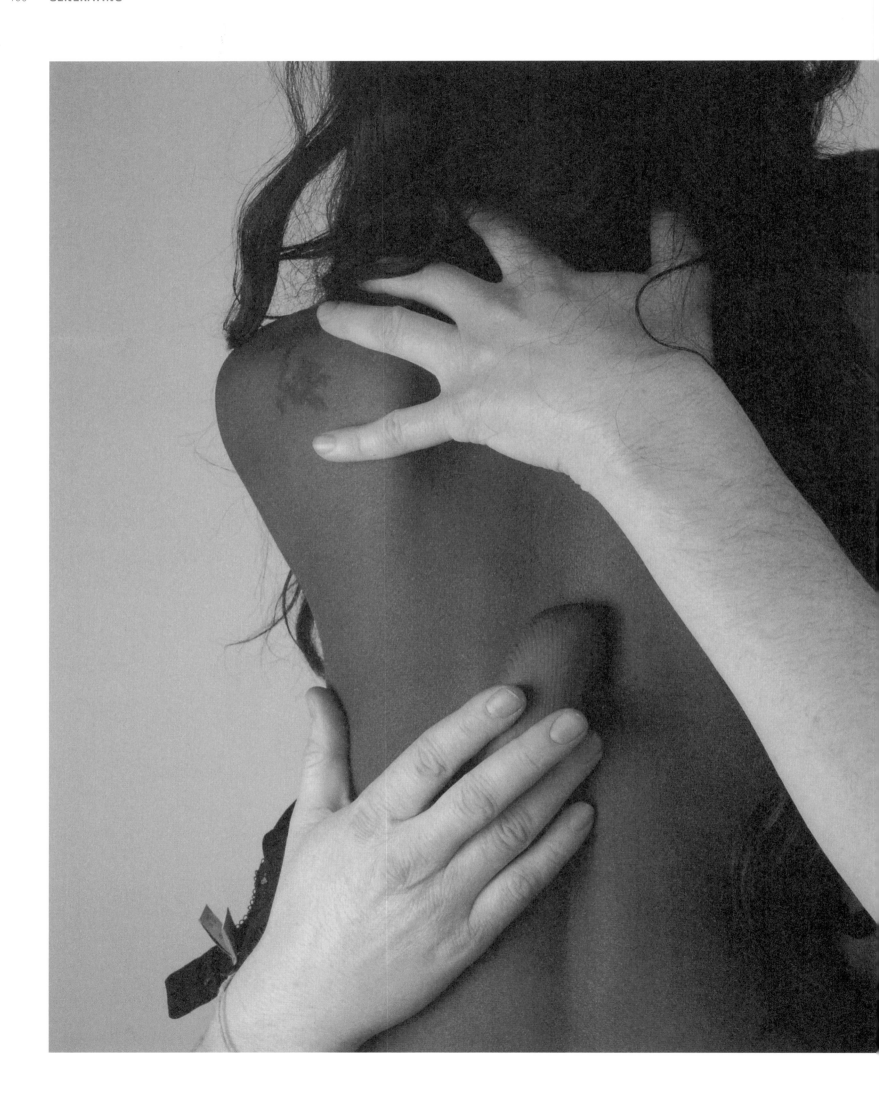

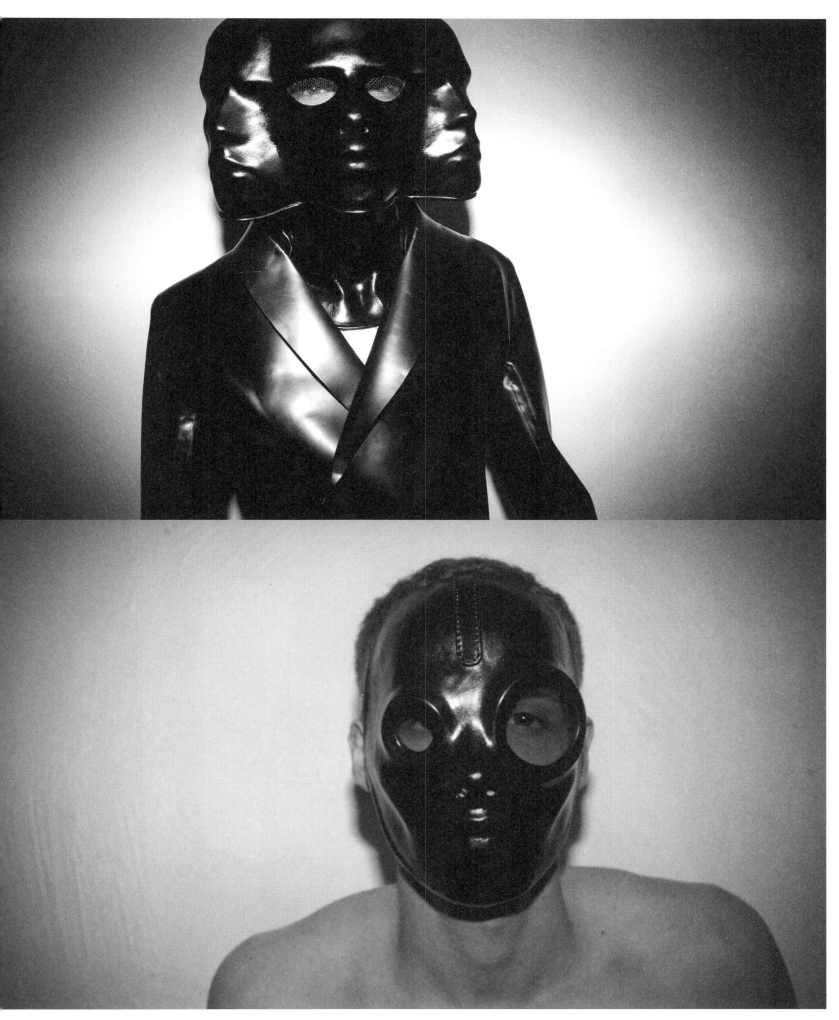

Opposite page: 'Woodvibes' by
Jonas Lönborg. Wood and brushed
amuminium

Top and bottom: 'The Impossibility of
Love' by Void of Course. A/W 2011–12

'Re.Treat #2' by Úna Burke.
Undyed vegetable-tanned Leather and
brass fittings

Opposite page: 'Re.Treat #4' by
Úna Burke. Undyed vegetable-tanned
Leather and brass fittings

'Lady Bell' by Noritaka Tatehana.
Lady Viola Museum A/W 2010–11.
Hand crafted leather

Opposite page: 'Shell Cup Puff
Sleeve Pencil Dress', 'Ultra Filigree
Choker', 'Beret' and 'Knuckle
Gloves' by Atsuko Kudo. Latex

'The Steel Heel' by Chau Har Lee.
Steel and leather

Opposite page: 'Gia Stockings'
by Bordelle. Elastic

Opposite page: 'Bleeding Heart' by
Solange Azagury-Partridge. 18ct yellow
gold and red lacquer

'Red Twist Platforms' by Gabriella
Marina Gonzalez. Leather

'The Petal Bra' by Coco de Mer.
2005. Silk

Opposite page: 'Harness and
Layered Clutch' by Fleet Ilya. SS11.
Leather

Exploring the 'O's:

"Electric flesh-arrows... traversing the body. A rainbow of color strikes the eyelids. A foam of music falls over the ears. It is the gong of the orgasm."
—Anais Nin

Orifice. Open. Orgasm. In exploring the O's we encounter objects, which play with, unlock, enhance, enter, travel and move inside essence. We seek the inner through the penetration of the outer. Within and without, without becomes within. Our mouth like openings, orifices revealed, in differing and varied flowering shapes and petals while others have full voluptuous lips and petals while others have barely any at all. Receptive passages leading into and through our bodies, united in their ability to take in, to embrace, to hold and contain. With open mouths we taste, appreciate and possess. The moment of essence, the moment from which we are from. A doorway opens to an O, opening into pleasured surrender.

We dilate and open and in opening we release and relinquish personal boundary. As the edges of ourselves dissolve we converge through touch, we meet, join and fuse.

It is here, in the non-emission state of pleasure, that our connection becomes richer, more full and intense. Immersed in the bliss of our desires, we are embraced in our fusion and the feelings of O reach and spread out into our conscious experience. No longer a singular and finite entity we are exposed, for we have blurred with and into another and into one another.

Until and eventually *la petite mort*, the little death. A moment of freedom and of everything and nothing-ness and of nothing-ness and everything. The heart beats faster, hastening, breathing quickening, the liberation of the life force, breathing becoming heavier, faster, the pounding pulse of pleasure. From deep inside to beyond the self, transcendence in a fleeting eternal moment comes as now. A climax in merging becomes an O inside and out. A sigh.

"...Your inside is out and your outside is in.
Your outside is in and your inside is out..."
—John Lennon

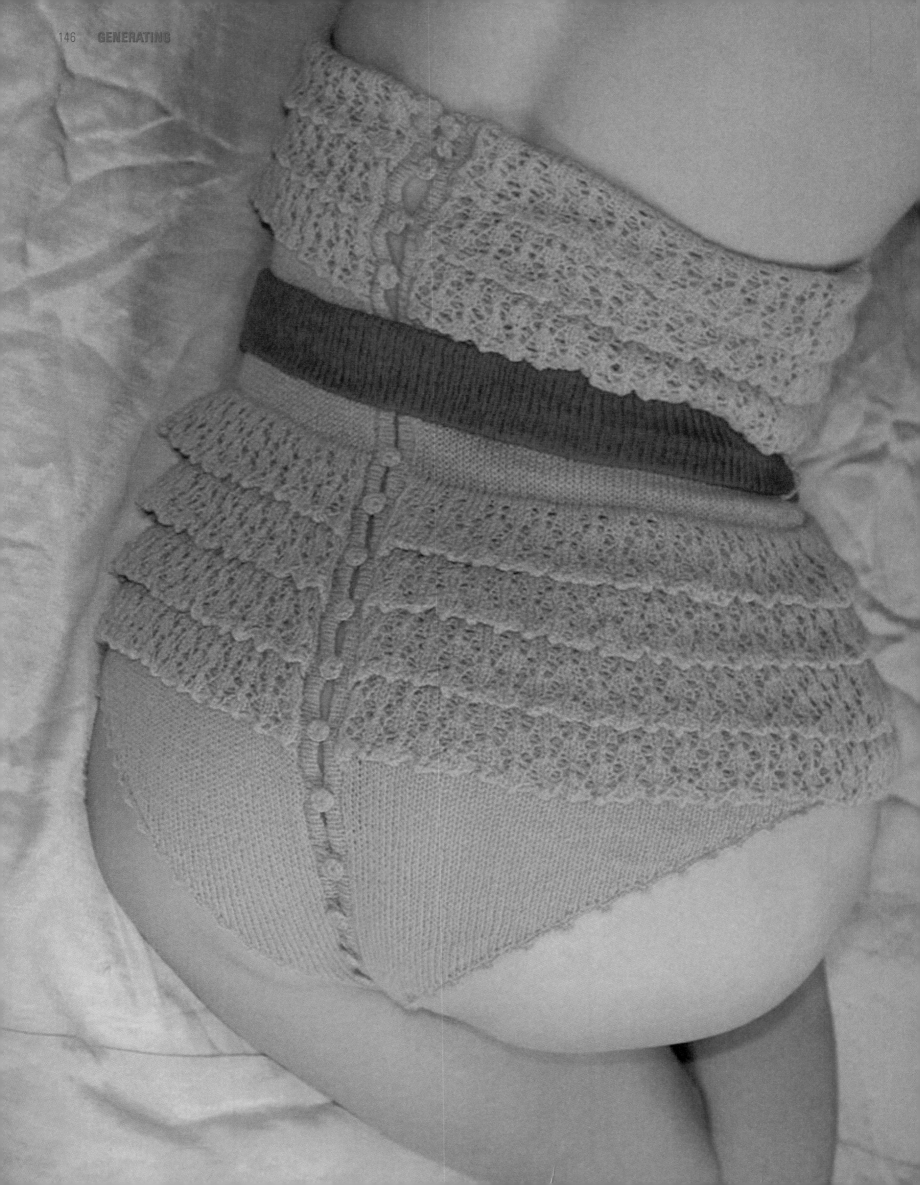

Opposite page: 'Mimi Gone High and Fluffy' by Strumpet & Pink. Cashmere

'Rose Bird Ceramic Butt Plug' by Coco de Mer in collaboration with Adele Brydges

Opposite page: 'Porcelain Geisha
Lips – Closed' by Coco de Mer

'Black Obsidian Anal Beads'
by Coco de Mer

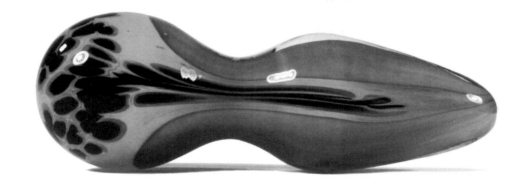

Opposite page: 'The Unicorn'
by Betony Vernon. Sterling silver
and horse hair

'Pink and Yellow Plug' by Shiri Zinn.
Glass

'Love Gun' by Betony Vernon.
Sterling silver

'Opposite Page: 'Girdle Skirt'
by Atsuko Kudo. Latex

'Red Strap' by Shiri Zinn. Nappa
leather, Chinese satin, beading

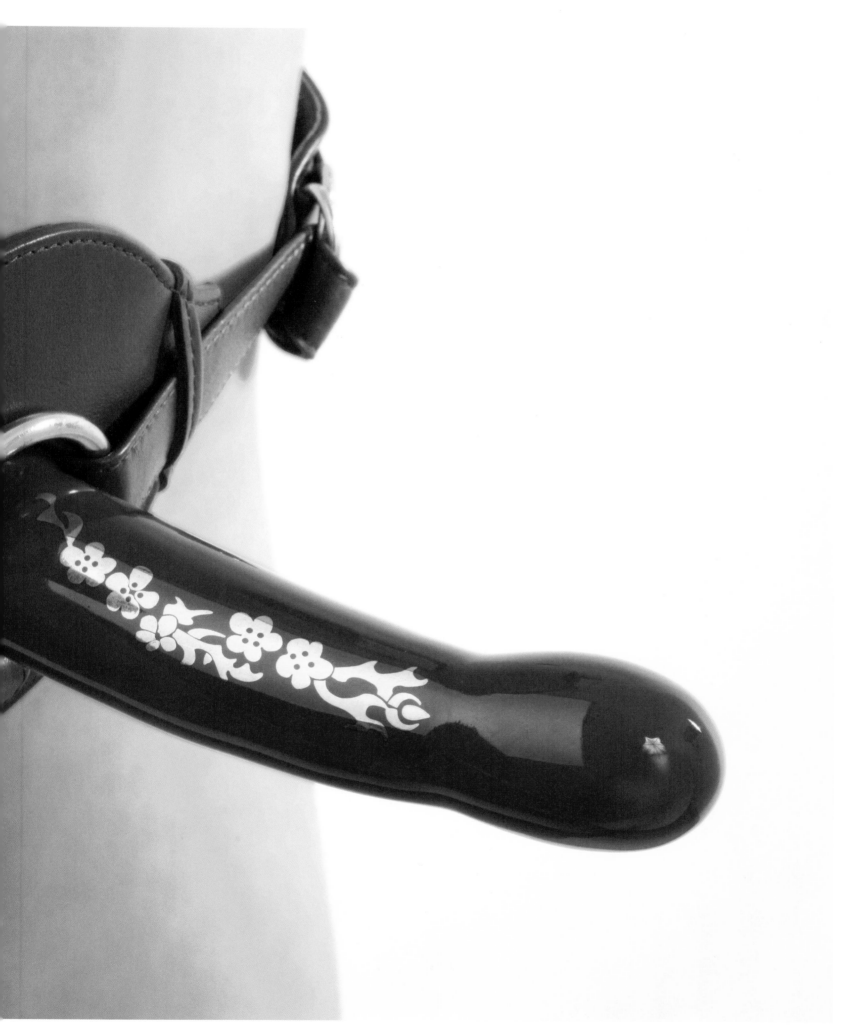

'Red Strap' with 'Red Ceramic Dildo' by
Shiri Zinn. Ceramic with 9 ct gold

'Avec Des Bas' by N De Samin. Silk

The Lake & Stars F/W 2010 Campaign

INTERVIEW WITH SHIRI ZINN

First object of desire: An empty Coke can. At seven years of age Shiri Zinn saw her best friend toying with an empty coke can and Shiri wanted this can very badly. She took it at the cause of great upset to her friend. Her father reprimanded Shiri with a huge spanking on the bum.

Shiri Zinn declares herself to be the inventor of the designer sex toy and of erotic couture. It is a wonderfully considered description of her artistry, which came into being almost by default.

Far from being inspired by fashion magazines, Shiri was reading and looking at health and the body from a female perspective when she became highly motivated by the statistics she found. She believes in the empowerment of a woman through her body, building and strengthening, as a means of developing inner expression and wisdom. When a woman knows and understands her body, a woman is able to direct her energies and knows how to locate and access her pleasure and, ultimately, knows how to be pleased. Shiri is a great believer in the body beautiful but her approach to this is rounded and holistic and very much to do with the process of working at, or toward, something with love.

This transformative approach, in particular, was fuelled by the desire to create an object of pure beauty out of that which is deemed ugly. It was here that she first created a quartz crystal dildo. This first piece, however, was as sharp as a razor and was connected to her fear of penetration and being sexually dominated. Coexisting at this time was the experience of a sexual blockage. It seems a curious contradiction as these objects appear, so emphatically, to be objects of and for desire and yet they were created from a subconscious space where physical desire was not fulfilled. However, through the repetitive process of polishing and streamlining this particular crystal piece, the razor-sharp became contoured, smooth, and as the object assumed usability, so too did the block transmute.

The proliferation of repugnant sex toys was ripe for the plundering of 'ugly' objects. Why in the world would you wish to penetrate the most female and interior part of yourself with something so visually and materially repellent? Although the development of ergonomically sound sex toys has improved the situation to a small degree, Shiri believes that the very fact these objects are so ergonomically 'sound' makes the whole act of sex too sanitixed and clean; promoting the clinical and hiding away or keeping hidden the luscious, visceral "sexiness."

Apart from the wealth of 'ugly' material potential available to Shiri in this area, she also chose to create sex toys as it allowed for a dynamic fusion or 'cross-over' between art, jewelry, fashion accessory and product design while allowing her the freedom to provoke. It was the perfect venue in which to shock because her creations were in such tremendous contrast to the products available. Shiri is able to make sexual or socio-political comments and feminist statements more directly while her artistry can be further demonstrated because her work straddles so many genres. She also cites her mother as her muse because she is "rather frigid and old-fashioned".

Shiri Zinn creates deliciously desirable, seductive and erotic objects, yet she claims to be a puritan. Perhaps she is more akin with a minimalist sensibility in as much as her pieces come from a point of purity of form and truth to material. She will work with a material that strikes and resonates with her in a particular way. Her ideas being explorations of a feeling or form combined with a defined focus on a tactile aesthetic. But it is her uncompromising and unyielding approach to her work, which is to be admired. Shiri is unrelenting about the quality of her work and is obsessive in its formulation. Yet, she does not create with an end in mind, the materials dictate the form and she is inwardly directed by the desire to create a piece with balance and composition. She has a conviction in her visual language that surprisingly is little to do with generating desire although, by default, her pieces inevitably do so. Her work is experiential in the fullest sense.

She has no desire to add to the mass of generic articles; churned out in the thousands under the guise of creating pleasure. The materials she chooses to use for her sex toys are inspired and connected to objects and techniques from antiquity. For example with the glorious red ceramic 'strap-on,' Shiri chose this material because she had been researching antique ejaculation bowls along with many other oriental erotic antiques. Ceramic was regularly used and she liked the qualities of the material combined with the fact that she was also able to fire 9-carat gold onto the piece. "I felt that if ceramic was safe enough to use for such intimate erotic pieces in antiquity they were certainly good enough for us."

Shiri Zinn frequently speaks of beauty and quoted Keats' Ode to a Grecian Urn 'Beauty is truth, truth beauty', "So you take the beauty and enjoy the beauty in it's purest form. With a person you take the beauty and you do not try to control it. The spiritual aspect comes in where integrity and truth unite and play. You can be opened up by beauty in its purest form for it is connected to ideals and principles." Beauty is more than a two dimensional plane for true beauty or an object of beauty touches all the internal points of registration and one is affected emotionally, spiritually and psychologically. It is through these qualities that Shiri Zinn is able to challenge prejudices and preconceived notions about sexuality.

'Gold Mirror Glass' by Shiri Zinn. Glass

Opposite page: 'Framboise' and
'L Cristal' Rosebuds by Julian Snelling.
Stainless steel and Swarovski

'Whip Bud' by Julian Snelling. Stainless
steel and leather

Opposite page: Jade Engraved Cock
Ring' by Coco de Mer. Carved in the
shape of Ouroborus – the serpent
who ate his own tail. Ouroborus is the
symbol of rebirth and continuity of life

'Jade Petite Fesse' by Coco de Mer.
Jade has always been associated
with sexuality and was traditionally
offered to the gods as a symbol of
enduring love.

'Night Slip' by Stephanie Loungewear.
Silk chiffon and tulle

Opposite page: 'Hot and Cold Ceramic
Dildo' by Coco de Mer in collaboration
with Adele Brydges

'THE TROPHY' BY BETONY VERNON

"A male G-spot stimulator. The male G-spot lies approximately 7 cm inside the anus and lower rectum and is more commonly known as the prostrate gland. Prostrate stimulation is related to prostate health so it is a good idea to get familiar with this part of your body, not only for a question of discovering its erotic power. The design of the Trophy is based on a medical tool for prostrate stimulation and due to its shape and size may be easily inserted into the anus. Lie in a relaxed position, on your back or side. Relaxation is the most important key to anal insertion. Use lube generously. The anus dilates with erotic pleasure so warm up with the help of your partner or on your own before you try to insert the tool. While holding the wider, larger curled motif of the curved handle towards you, insert the trophy. Once the object is in place this wide curl will press against the perineum, the sensitive area between the testicles and the anus. Learning to control the sphincter muscles, which hold the tool in place, will put you on the path to anal health and ecstasy. Be patient with your body, take time out to explore and you will be rewarded. Do not move the trophy with penetrative gestures, simply put it in place and let the tool do the rest however feel free to masturbate or make love."

'The Trophy' by Betony Vernon.
Sterling silver

"Ben Wa Balls" by Betony Vernon. Sterling silver. *"Serve to enhance the pleasures of female masturbation as well as the mutual joys of penetration."*

Opposite page: 'Spirit of Ecstasy' by Mark Woods 1999. Carved phenolic acid plastic, gold plated silver, synthetic rubies

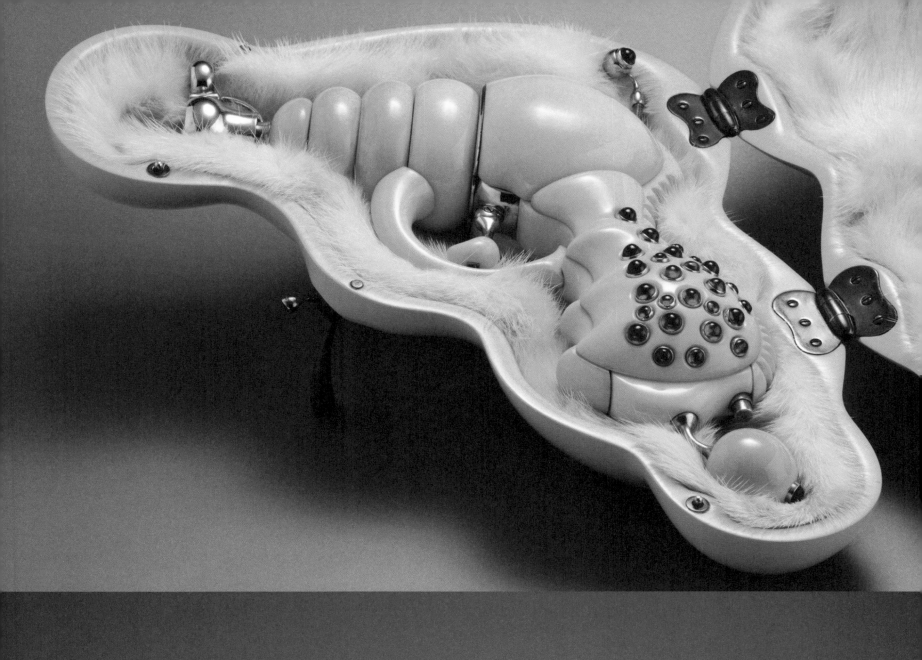
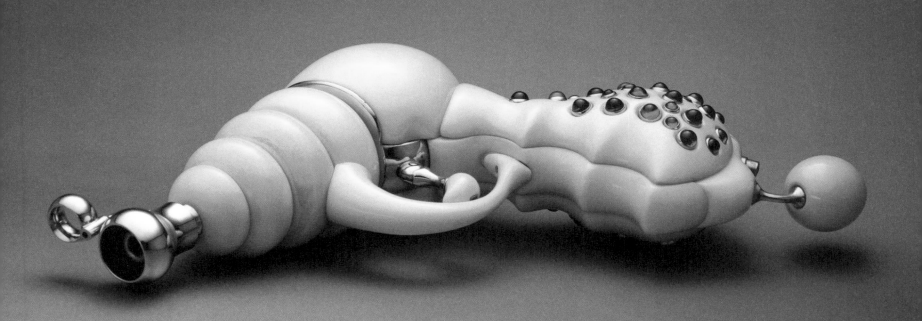

CONTEMPLATING DESIRE

I vividly recall my adolescent encounter with a fur cup and saucer (and a teaspoon). A simple object, so very familiar and reassuringly recognizable in the everyday and yet, it was utterly absurd, unexpected and extraordinary. It amused and enthralled with its *Alice in Wonderland* curiosity and simultaneously bestowed a frisson that was both suggestive and rude. I wanted to touch it.

But had the tactile understanding of *Luncheon in Fur* been consummated would my emotional recognition or desire for the piece remain the same? For in my minds eye, the palpable experience of fingering and stroking the inner curve of silky fur was so full that perhaps the reality would fall short. The fur may be stiff or there could well be a residue of hard and displeasing glue.

In Contemplating desire the majority of the pieces in this section, as with most artworks, can only be felt and touched with the visual mind and through the internal points of registration, for, predominantly, direct physical engagement is not encouraged or permitted. In working with desire as a concept, does this indeed make the emotional connection and understanding of craving and longing all the more vivid and real? Desire as demonstration, enriched and roused because there is no corporeal conclusion or finite end. The tangible experience can never be fulfilled and we are confronted with the ambiguity of desire. Wanting and longing become amplified for the object of desire can only be grasped in the imagination as absence filled.

Conflicting emotions are set into play for many artists seduce our visual desires and we perceive an aesthetic pleasure as purity, which is an emotional reality, but ultimately we are kept at a physical distance and are less aware of the irregularities and imperfections in a forms idealized surface. We may desire more because we only see perfection.

"There are two tragedies in life. One is not to get your heart's desire. The other is to get it."
–George Bernard Shaw, Man and Superman

Within this section however, there are also pieces, which are categorised as fashion or design, objects made wearable or created with physical connection in mind. They not only work with desire as a concept and seduce our visual pleasure centers but the fundamental aspect in creating their visual language and understanding is based on our tangible and desirable experience of them. How we fit into them, how they feel against our skin and how desire is communicated with and by our bodies. It is the relationship between these objects and our physical selves that is not only encouraged but also implicit in their comprehension. Is this what differentiates a piece of design or a work of art, the aspect of our physical engagement? It has little to do with production or rarity or unique-ness as the majority of the design pieces are created as one-offs or as limited runs. We have to question whether an object or 'piece' that is sensed and understood with the physicality of ourselves is deemed as 'less than' due to the fact that we still perceive our bodies and physical selves as base. Traditional "fine art" pieces are elevated to a position of eminence for they are taken-in without proximity and we are forbidden to touch.

In contemplating desire we see how different artists and designers explore desire as a concept, and assimilate Eros into their visual language and how longing, love, pleasure and lust are made manifest. Desire has the capacity to embody quite contradictory and, at times, unpleasant emotions and many of the concepts made perceptible convey a characteristic or quality which could be defined as a slippage between that which seduces and that which repels; an erotic attraction mixed with a deliberate perversity.

The conflicting emotions and experiences that become or define desire are universal but it is how we engage with them or find and discover meanings and significance, which matters. The path of desire and the investigation of it will ultimately lead us to an exploration or uncovering, and a discovery of the self.

"When I was a child Meret Oppenheim secreted her teacups somewhere in the back of my mind cupboard. Sometimes I take them out for mad tea parties I have with my selves and my creatures."

– Midori

'Luncheon in Fur' by Meret Oppenheim 1936.
Fur-covered cup, saucer, and spoon

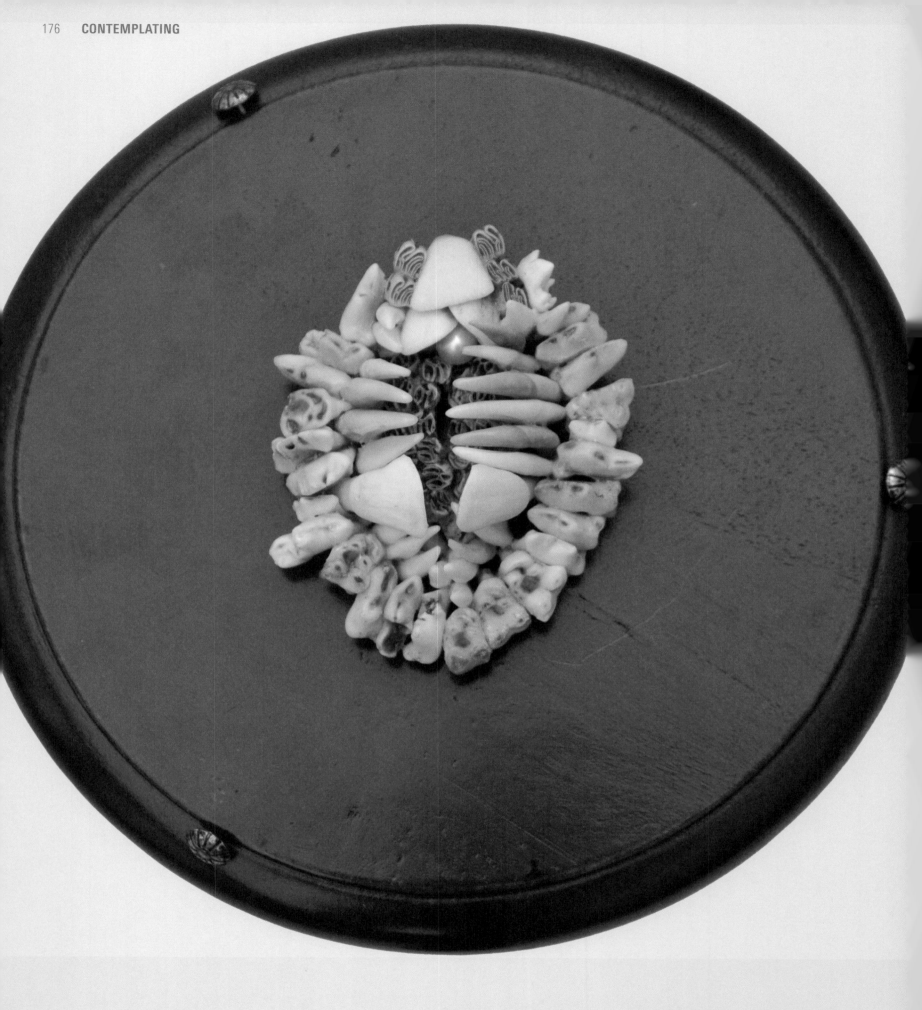

'Object 0' (detail) by Midori

Opposite page: 'Object Cluster: Object 0, Object 1, Object 1.1' by Midori 2011. Medium: small animal teeth, wood, glass dome, brass nails, hunger, brass hook, cotton thread, glass apothecary jar, rabbit fur, pig leather, dehydrated corn cob granules, philosophunculism, brass hooks, rabbit fur, pig leather, antique velvet box, dehydrated corn cob granules, venialia

ANNIE ATTRIDGE:

Annie Attridge uses the ornamental and seductive qualities of porcelain to explore Baroque traditions of figurative decorative sculpture. Her works are fused with private dramas of desire and longing and contain underlying waves of passion, sinuous love triangles, romantic archetypes combined with comic symbolism. Exploiting the medium's potential to be modelled, stretched, decorated with colored glazes, Attridge creates entangled, orgiastic, and amorphous scenes that resonate playfully with sensual pleasures. The work itself becomes both object and a sign of desire. The work "Love Thrills" symbolizes two lovers embracing, unbound by the constraints of social regulations and rules. The arrow as the principal weapon echoes the verse of Virgil's famous phrase: "Love conquers all, let us yield to love. "

Attridge explains: "I was told once, 'Annie, always chose a subject that turns you on,' and so my love for my materials is crucial: I choose them with an eye to their erotic potential. Getting my hands right in there, wet clay nurtured with a labor of love slowly turns into hard clay."
—Statement courtesy of Asya Geisberg Gallery 2011

'Love Thrills' by Annie Attridge 2011.
Porcelain with enamel glaze, pewter
spire 20cm x 19cm x 16cm. Spire 14cm.
Collection of George Yacoumatos

Opposite page top: 'Breast Horse' by Annie Attridge 2010. Detail from 'Your Borders, Your Rivers, Your Tiny Villages'. Porcelain with enamel glaze 13 cm x 15cm x 16cm. Private Collection

Opposite page bottom: 'Your Borders, Your Rivers, Your Tiny Villages' by Annie Attridge 2010. Porcelain with enamel glaze on ping pong table, 73.5cm x 155cm x 137cm. Courtesy of Asya Geisberg Gallery

'Hybreed' by Charlotte Kingsnorth. Chair and neoprene skin

'Hybreed' by Charlotte Kingsnorth.
Chair and velvet

Opposite page: 'At One - the loveseat'
by Charlotte Kingsnorth. Latex, foam
and ash

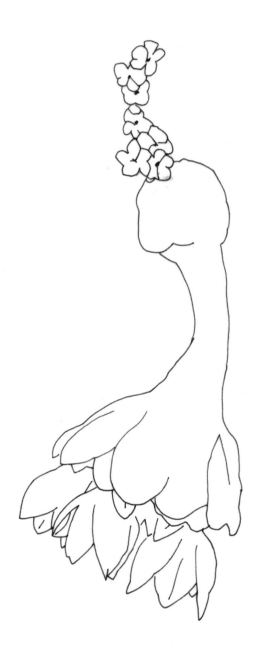

Opposite page: 'Clematitis Allium
Burst' by Stephanie Q Rubin 2004.
Pen on tracing paper

'Consoladores' by Stephanie Q Rubin
2004. Cast glass

'Marie Coquine' by Philippe Starck. In the manner of a cheeky, bouncy, sexy tale, Philippe Starck has designed a gravity-defying floor chandelier for Baccarat. Marie Coquine, for that's her name, colourfuly combines a marriage of convenience with an invitation to dreamland. Mary Poppins squaring up Raging Bull in a ring corner. And when the two meet, Marie Coquine deploys all her grace, at once fragile and strong, perfectly balanced and subtly anchored to the ground. With her stunning build, and a figure to break the hearts of poets, this variation on the Zénith 12L chandelier has inspired Philippe

Starck a subtle battle of wills. Under its ivory umbrella and with its crystal ribs articulated around a telescopic illusion, the chandelier version seems to float in mid-air, radiant and replete. Perched atop a photographic stand, the Zénith floor light is ready to take off, simply counterweighted by a Camel leather punching ball. Sheer spatial magic. And the light, singing in the rain, transforms fantasy into reality. Naughty and nice, Marie Coquine.

Opposite page: 'Lipstick' wallpaper by Paper Voyeur

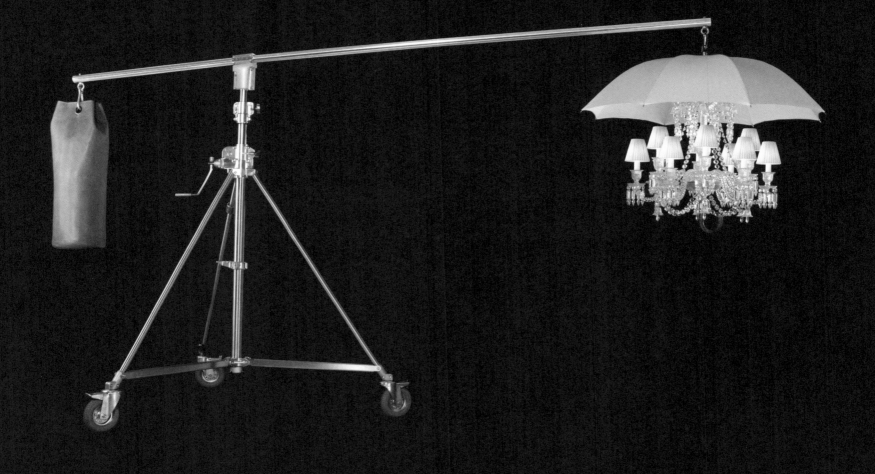

'Spent' by Michael Petry 2004. Silver coins. For this work Petry melted his childhood silver coin collection, pouring it out to resemble a large ejaculate. It speaks of childhood and the passage into adulthood, the physical changes that allow boys to become men, yet is still merely spilled metal. The work is loaded with autobiographical information, yet the melting of the collection into a mass, reduces the whole to a mass of memories

'BB108' by Michael Petry 2009. Glass and silver plated object at Sir John Soane's Museum, London 2010. Petry's Bare Back Lovers series of poured glass sculptures are all called BB works and are given the number in the sequence of their making. As in unprotected sex, hot fluid is poured into an open receptacle

Opposite page: Top left: 'Horsehair
Mattress' by Daniel Heer. Fine horse
hair and stitched by hand
Bottom left 'Dpot' by Jum Nakao
Pine transport box, golden chains,
capitone leather, foam, light.
140cm x 50cm x 210cm

'MAP Unit' by Michael Petry 2000.
Freshwater pearls the length of Petry's
height, silver clasp. The work can be
worn as a performance art worked
called 'Wearing Michael Petry's Pearl
Necklace', alluding to the sexual practice of a man ejaculating onto another's
chest. Detail on following page

'MAP Unit' (detail) by Michael Petry

William's Voice' by Michael Petry 2003. Laminated photo, antique oil can. It alludes to William S. Burroughs' seminal work *Naked Lunch* (1959), where the main character, William Lee, a writer/ secret agent uses many drugs to finish his novel/accomplish his missions. He hallucinates that his typewriter has turned into a talking bug whose mouth resembles a giant anus, and demands that Lee massage drugs into its sphincter in order to type.

Opposite page: 'Bad Seed 1' by
Michael Petry 2011. Yellow Murano
glass on a period sofa at Sir John
Soane's Museum, London

'Randy' by Michael Petry 2008. A
melted and reformed one ounce 22ct
gold South African Krugerrand, from
Petry's Spill series

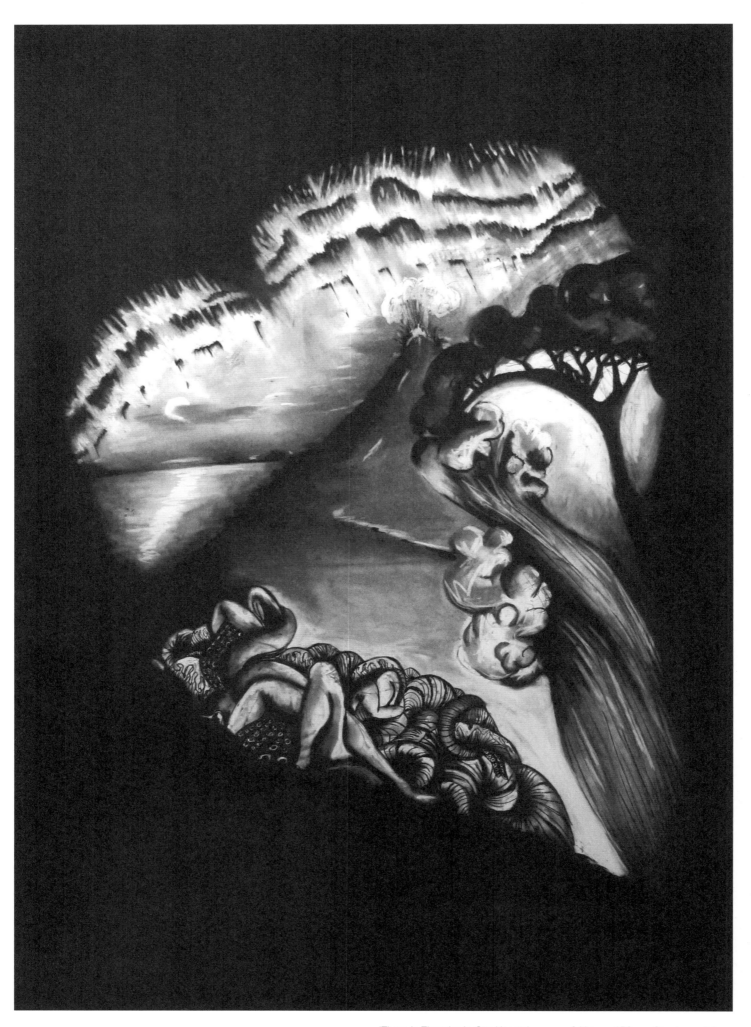

'There is Thunder in Our Hearts' by Annie Attridge 2008. Compressed charcoal on Fabriano paper.

241cm x 150cm. Courtesy of Asya Geisberg Gallery

'Hand-printed silk corset'
by Jane Wildgoose © 1985

"PINK-NESS NO.6". EDITION OF 100.

The intention behind communicating pink-ness in a non-visual manner liberated this rosy hue from its more manufactured and debased, exterior, associations, such as Barbie, candy floss and bubble gum. I sensed that an odour could make manifest my feeling of the pink as it has the ability to capture emotion and access the vernacular of bodily or instinctive understanding. Smells pass into and out of our bodies, tracing our internal landscape with their tides. Spatially, within the scent itself, I wanted there to be tiers of permeating aromatics, so that the scent moved and developed as one engaged with it, shifting with time and temperature. The first intake of breath should have an emergent powdery waft, doused with a heady odour of rose. This more literal association towards pink was a means to disarm, to dilute resistance to the approaching intimate experience. The scent awakens with the temperature of the body and it slowly ascends to a deep and visceral fecund pink. The sexual smell of bodies merging and being sensorially open. One could converge with its fragrance as much in the groin as in the solar plexus. At this point, one no longer thinks of pink 'things', rather one comes to know the pink via direct internal experience.

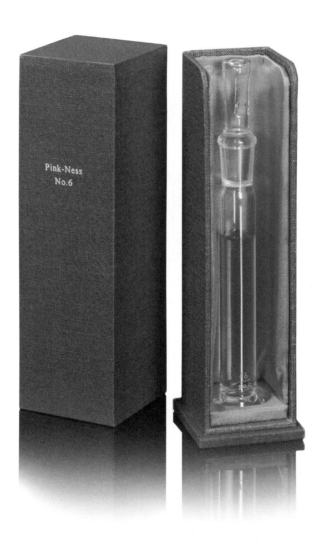

'Pink-ness No. 6' by Lisa Z Morgan 2001.
14cm x 4cm x 4cm

'Bocca' by Fornasetti

'Rose Chair' by Edra and designed
by Masanori Umeda 1990. Rose-
shaped, it can be seen as a haute
couture item. The petals, which
form the padding and make the seat
welcoming, are hand made one by one

'REVENGE OF THE FLORIST' BY MICHAEL PETRY

Petry's exhibition 'Revenge of the Florist' (Westbrook Gallery, London, 2009) presented his Nature Mort series of coloured blown glass and cut flowers which include the fourth dimension of time. Paintings of still lives attempted to bring time into them by depicting decay (rotting fruits, meat) and the mortality of the viewer (skulls). Petry's works allow the viewer to see decay in real time. The cut flowers slowly lose their bloom, their beauty fading. Each vessel speaks several coded languages based on its colour (based on the 1970's gay hanky code: purple for spanking, orange for 'anything goes') and the flowers (hyacinths for forgiveness, roses for love, ect.). Each receptacle is unique, and is a portrait of someone's anus. Petry invited men and women on the internet to send an image of their sphincter for the basis of a portrait. These works appear as simple floral arraignments in pretty vases, but are also sexually explicit portraits that change before the viewer's eyes

'Orange/Any' by Michael Petry 2009,
blown glass, cut flowers, fresh state

'The Octopus Chair' by Máximo Riera 2010

'Chair' by Maarten Baptist. Red
birch wood

Opposite page: 'Dressing Up'
by Augustus Goertz. Liquid light

Opposite page: 'The Sock' by Augustus
Goertz. Liquid light

'Octopussy' by Kiki Smith 1998.
17.8cm x 16.5cm x 5.1cm. Phosbronze

'Quilt – The Thing' by Ronan & Erwan
Bouroullec 2011

Opposite page: 'A Bouquet for
the Duchess of Portland' by Jane
Wildgoose © 2009. Sugar and
shell flowers

'Irradiance' by Jan Taminiau F/W 2011

Opposite page: 'Fragile-Flow Blud'
by Kim Joon 2010. Digital print
120cm x 120 cm.
"Kim Joon uses the technique of "skin-
ning" against perfected illusion and to-
ward an erotic but uncanny dislocation.
In doing so the artist undermines the
value of conformity in both embodiment
and consumption. These bodies are
not sealed packages, they are uneven
surfaces reflecting our conflicted self-
creation—in the artist's words; "multi-
layered composites of desire and will,
emotion and action, pain and pleasure
of self and other... a complex system of
complicit activities"

Opposite page: 'Dalston Rose Victorian
Conversation Chair' by House of
Hackney

'Soda' by Paper Voyeur

'Pants (for Hiding)' by Eric Magnuson   Opposite page: 'Women 25'
1991. Canvas, zipper, hanger.   by Fileti © 2009
182.8cm x 55.8cm x 55.8cm

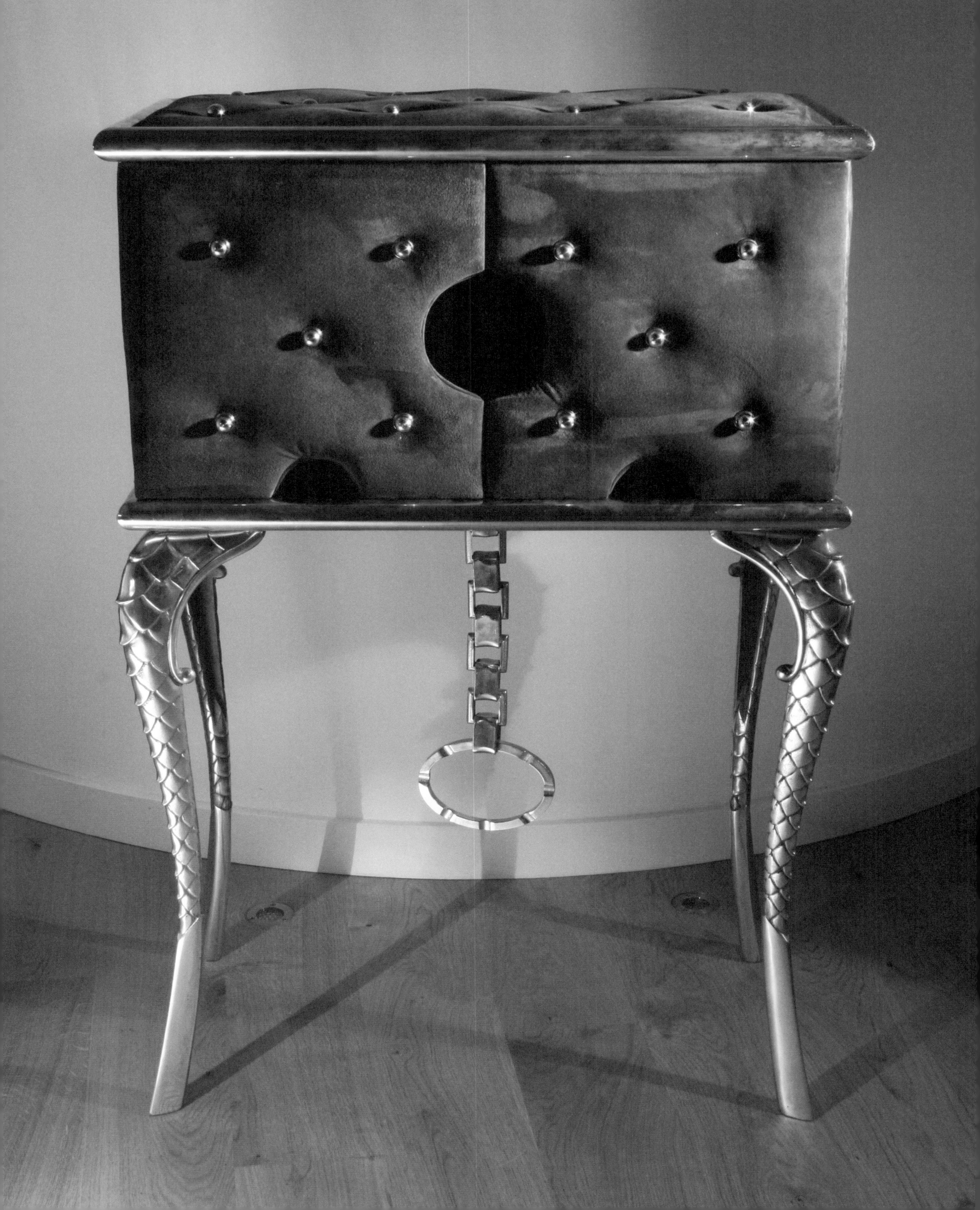

Jo Nagasaka for Llove Hotel, Tokyo. The 6 C-type rooms consist of three sets of two neighboring rooms. The guests of these sets can enjoy an 'unrelated connection' through the subtle mechanisms in these rooms. Every set has its own theme: *'misunderstanding', 'overwriting'* and *'misinterpretation'*

'HOLE STORY' TROU STORY BY EMMANUELLE WAECKERLE

"A simple construction of a monumental hole in diminishing perspective emphasised by the play of light on the torn paper. Each hole has been lovingly perforated using various parts of my body as drilling tools.

A blank space, awaiting meaning and interpretation. Some have seen endings, bottomless void, bullet wound, flesh, open mouth; others beginnings, pleasure domw, abstraction, gateway, siphon......
A hole is a home is a hole is a home
My hole is your home is my hole is your home"

'Hole Story' *trou story* by Emmanuelle Waeckerle 2006. Installation. Seven frames of 240cm x 200cm

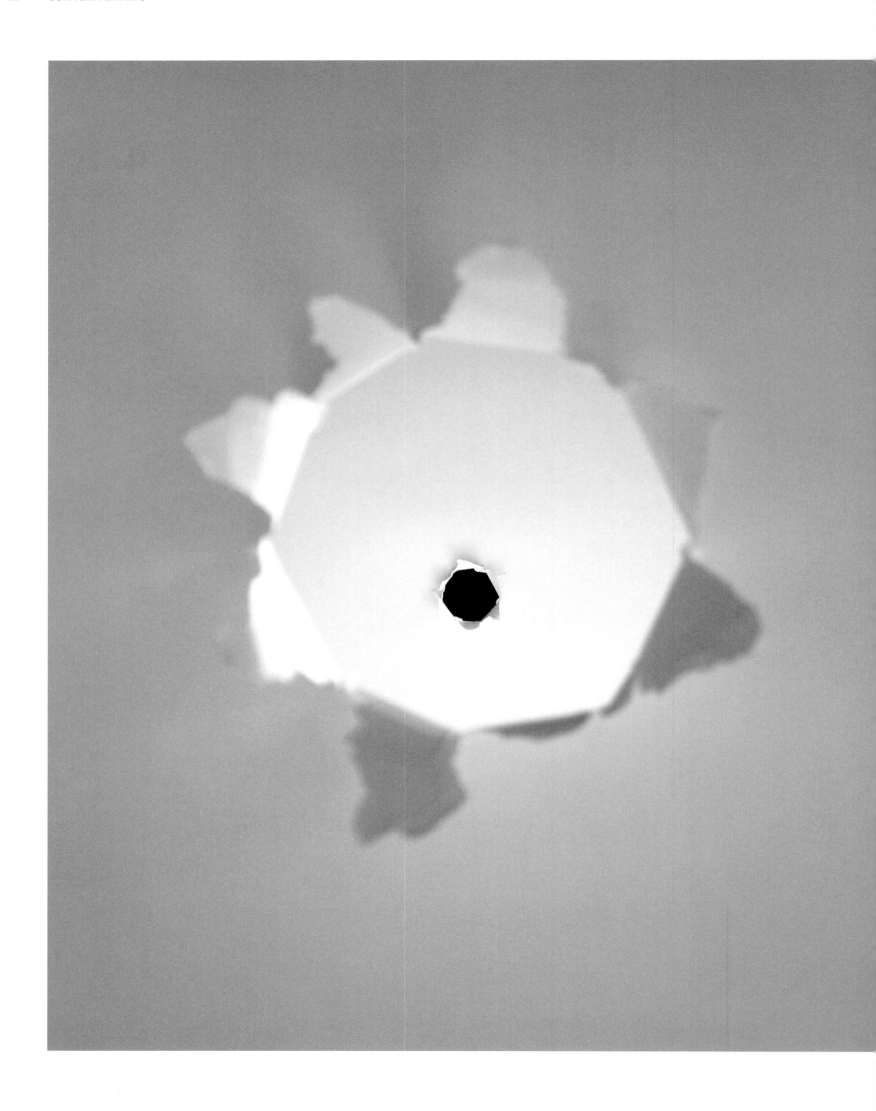

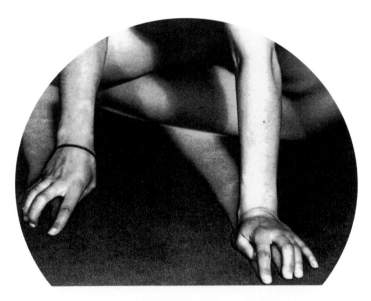

Natacha, 1931

Opposite page: 'Hole Story' trou story
by Emmanuelle Waeckerle 2006.
Installation (detail).
7 frames of 240cm x 200cm

'Natacha (Man Ray)' by Giorgio Sadotti
2006. Photograph

'Hatstand (Allen Jones)' by Giorgio
Sadotti 2006. Photograph

29

'Hair, fur' by Bruno Grizzo 2009.
Collage

Opposite page: 'Hands and Feet'
by Bruno Grizzo 2009. Collage

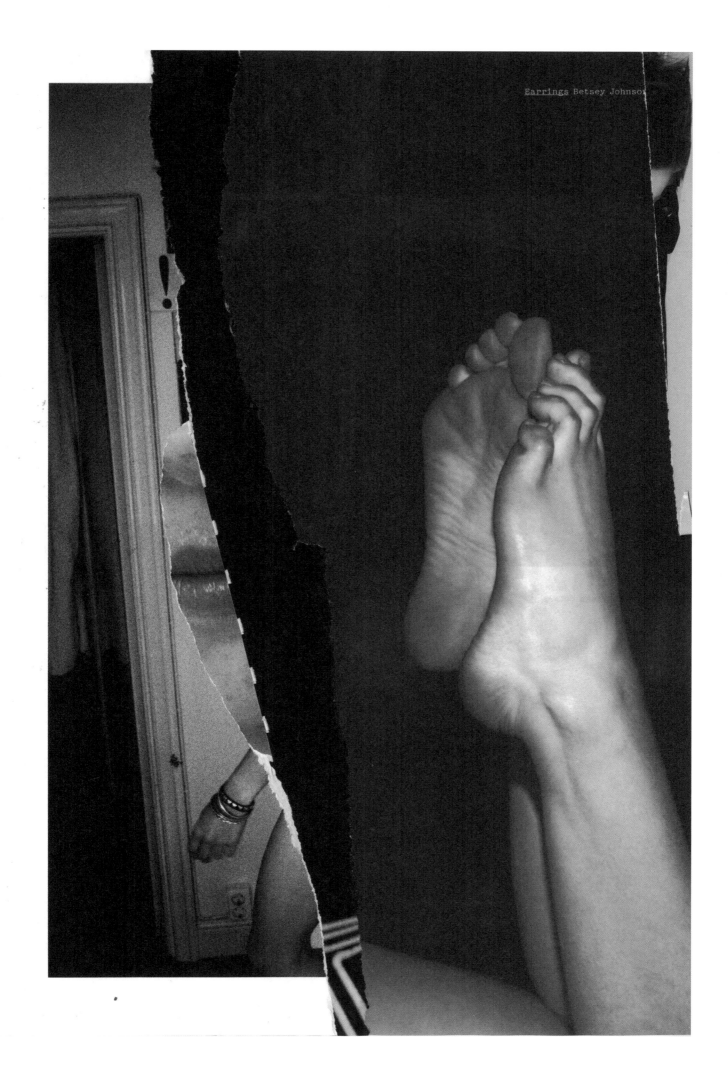

Earrings Betsey Johnson

'Women 13' by Fileti © 2009

Opposite page: 'Unicorn' by Noritaka Tatehana. Phantom 2011. Hand crafted leather with gold metal thorns

'Imitation Leather Cape Dress' by Junya Watanabe Comme des Garçons. A/W 2010–11. Courtesy of Comme des Garçons

Top: 'Kill 'em all, God will know his own' by Mark Woods 2009. Rhodium plated silver, leather. 175mm x 125mm x150mm

Bottom: 'A Sundry Female Object' by Mark Woods 2003. Silver, leather, lace. 250mm x120mm x 65mm

Opposite page: 'Aleister Crowley' by Grow House Grow. *"This wallpaper pattern stems from the summer of 1938, which Crowley spent in Cornwall. Some unsubstantiated sources site cultish melees involving dancing beauties, hard narcotics and evenings spent in black magic debauchery."*

'Forget-Me-Not' Wallpaper 2001.
Concept Peter Saville. Illustration Julie
Verhoeven. Design Paul Hetherington.
An interactive installation commissioned
by SHOWstudio. The design makes
explicit references to Japanese rope
suspension bondage in a French Toile
de Jouy style

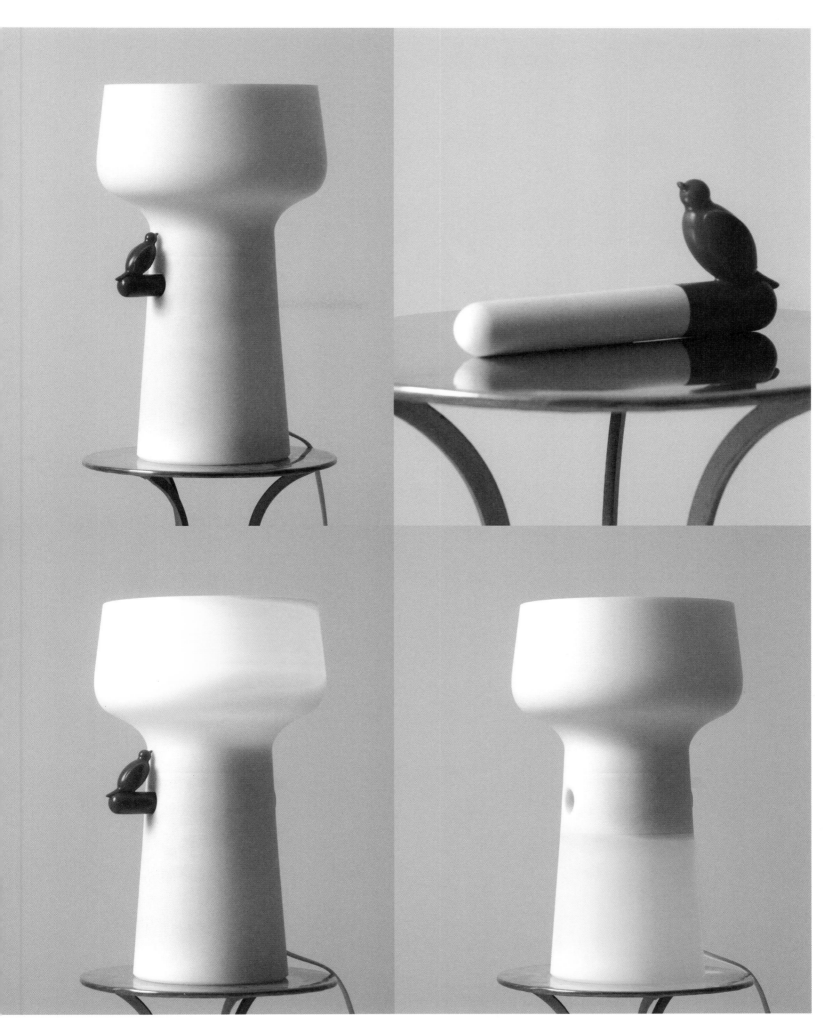

'Love the Bird' by Marc Dibeh

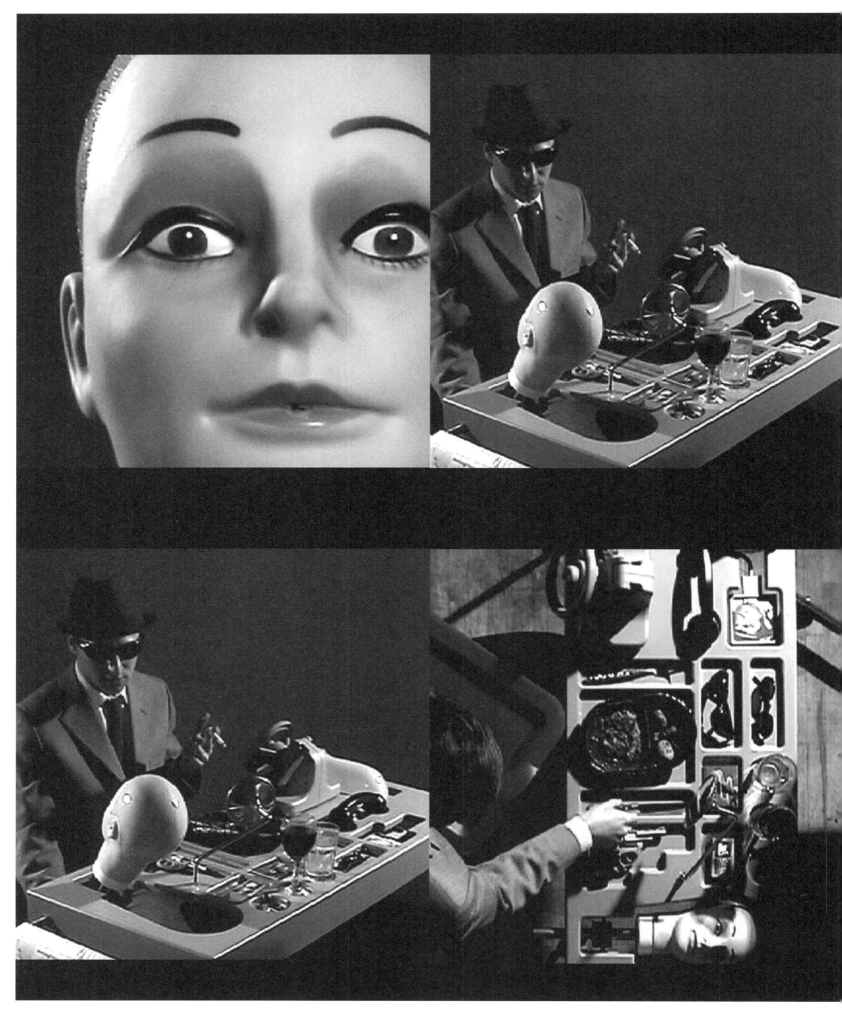

Stills from 'Object for Lonely Men'
by Noam Toran 2001

'Last Night I Dreamed…' by Patrycja
Domanska 2010. Installation (detail).
Mixed-media

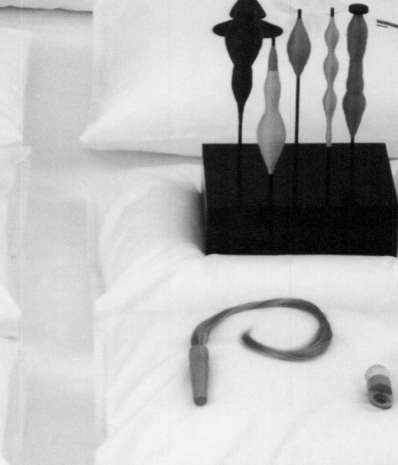

last night I dreamed...

'Last Night I Dreamed…' by Patrycja Domanska 2010. Installation Mixed-media. *"An attempt to explore the sexuality of daily objects. The most basic parameters of design like form, dimension, material, surface and* combinations of objects trigger very individual associations with people. There are no descriptions guiding through, in order to still allow for the subjectivity of eroticism and sexuality."

Opposite page: 'Re.Treat #5' by Úna Burke. Undyed Vegetable-tanned leather and brass fittings

INTERVIEW WITH MARC ATLAN

First object of desire: His father's cigar cutter, a small object like a guillotine in highly polished gold. Marc was fascinated by the function of the object. A sharp blade within a hole creates a special incision in the cigar. It was a beautiful, perfect tool, and almost assumed the guise of jewelry.

In his early teenage years Marc Atlan spent much time at his grandparents. His grandmother, although blind, was very concerned about her looks and she was, he says "very coquettish." She had a wonderful collection of make-ups from Guerlain and Chanel and he was attracted and drawn to the beautiful packaging. He would immerse himself and spend hours perusing the containers and boxes, the colors, powdery scents and particularly the instructions, in tiny type, and different languages. Objects were explored with a fascination that verged on the fetishistic. Time stretched as he said, "minutes felt like hours and immortality was evident." A seed was undoubtedly planted during these syrupy hours.

The Fashion Institute of Technology in New York invited Marc Atlan, along with many other artists and celebrities, to create an art work, an artistic statement about the fragrance industry and the world of perfume. The perfumed world was and is Marc's creative field. He has worked and designed for almost every major fashion designer and fashion house in the industry. But the idea to create his own fragrance was never an obvious desire, rather more a subliminal dream. "Like day dreaming; I liked the idea."

He was given the word 'disaster' to work with. Immediately, he was semantically resounding with the word; 'disaster' – death, mort in French, le petite mort, 'the little death', orgasm. The idea was fully formed. The moment he hung up the phone he could see the bottle in his mind's eye and he knew how it would smell. "It was almost as though it already existed".

A perfume takes around 18-24 months to come to fruition. Marc had four months in which to make manifest his idea. It was time for him to dive into his vision of what he wanted to create. "I wanted to replicate, not the smell of the female genitals, but the smell of something more complex." He could very easily obtain a sample of blood, or urine, "for a man to jerk off I would get the sperm." All these bodily fluids were easily attainable. "I wanted something more intricate and this had to come from a woman." There is a fluid, which a woman secretes when she is sexually aroused. This has a bodily function in providing lubrication prior to penetration. But it is only created when the woman's desire is awakened otherwise the fluid will not materialize. "You cannot force that – it is remarkable." Marc

was fascinated by the idea that "there is a bodily fluid that is secreted by desire, it means there is a particular chemistry taking place in the brain of the woman. Men are just not made like that."

Facilitated by his friend Kilian Hennessy, Marc was introduced to Bertrand Duchaufour, "basically a rock star in the perfume industry," who will readily decline any job where innovative compromise is entailed. Having read Marc's concept, to create the scent of the bodily fluid that a woman secretes when she is about to climax, was far too tempting a project for Bertrand to refuse. It seems he would have paid for such a brief. "I was not attempting to invent an elixir of desire." Quite simply, it was his personal interpretation or replication of a particular aspect of desire and he wanted to express it through the medium of scent. "It is not a fragrance it is an art work that uses the vocabulary of fragrance or, you could say, it is a fragrance that uses the vocabulary of an art work." It is not readily identifiable and he loves objects that cannot be categorized. Using a scent to convey an idea removes any visual preconceptions. On breathing in, the perfume is drawn inside and here you are able to create your own internal images; finding connections and meaning through memory.

As a boy he saw the 1974 Italian movie Scent of a Woman, with his blind grandmother. He was inspired and also acutely aware that when one cannot see with the eyes, the other senses become highly developed and finely attuned. "To recognize someone, a woman by her smell alone, was profoundly moving and I wanted to create this experience in a perfume." The idea being, "not to wear something, but to wear somebody". The scent therefore had to be the scent from one woman. Hence, the beautiful play on words Parfum d'une Femme - Perfume from a woman. Marc found a woman who was deeply in love and also in a state of deep desire. He collected the fluid of arousal, a task in itself, in an un-sterilized jam jar. The sample was sent to Bertrand.

What developed was a scent that becomes more interesting with time, developing and evolving as the base notes warm with the skin. There are layers within the fragrance while at the same time being almost transparent. "You cannot really decipher what it smells like, you struggle to define it. You cannot say that it is peppery or floral, or anything in particular." It is an alchemical mix of synthetic and natural ingredients and "appeals to both men and women whether you are a prude or not. People were expecting something repulsive, but it is not because it connects with your inner primal self." Petite Mort somehow becomes part of your body. You know it and yet it is unknown, familiar and yet foreign. You find yourself part of it but are compelled to return to meet it; like the perfect lover. One woman who wore Petite Mort likened the experience to inhaling the t-shirt of her boyfriend by day after their night of sex. Another said "it was as though somebody had licked me."

The concept for Petite Mort blends literature with physics, the alchemical with eroticism in a pure artistic gesture. What Marc has developed is the antithesis of all that takes place in the perfume world and in an industry, which is fuelled and founded on sexuality and attraction. Yet, what he has created has infuriated perfumers, reporters and bloggers alike. Why? Because Petite Mort is the antithesis of titillation and disassociation. What he has created is charged and sexual. It is, in essence, arousal and sex undiluted and it has shocked. It says a great deal about the perceptions toward sex and sexuality when it is in full concentration; potent and loaded.

And it is concentrated. So concentrated it is viscous. Most perfumes contain 10%–40% of aromatic compounds. Petite Mort contains 100%. The dosage: a single drop. The color is a deep purple, almost black with a mercurial flash. A color attuned to Marc's psyche. It contains minute shimmering particles, almost undetectable to the naked eye, a galaxy in miniature, suspended perfectly in the thick fluid. "Everything about the perfume is extreme, it is extremely small, it is extremely limited, it is extremely expensive." The volume content of the bottle is 10 milliliter and the bottle stands just three centimetres 'tall'. Created in a limited edition of 100, the bottle costs $1000. Once Petite Mort is gone it is gone.

Marc believes that sexual desire is a taboo, the thing that people do not speak about. "It is like masturbating, farting, taking a shit, fucking - yet we all do it. But there is the desire which goes beyond the bodily function, it is not necessary but life would be miserable without it." He has found that Petite Mort seems to 'work' on everybody, probably because desire is universal. "It is something we all want, that which drives us. Our everyday would be pointless without desire."

The project was completed in only three months however Marc felt something else was required. He knew how he felt about the perfume but was curious to know how others perceived it; to have someone else's vision. He invited artists and designers, who have been instrumental in making him who he is today, to contribute their thoughts about Petite Mort. Andres Serrano, renowned for his work with bodily fluids, created an image; Rankin produced a powerful triptych. Almost everybody who has been invited to participate has given so much of themselves. Perhaps this is connected to the fact that the process and vision are integral and without compromise.

Marc says that he learns a lesson with each and every job or project he works on. Some projects are a nightmare from beginning to end and everything that can go wrong will. The creation of Petite Mort and the life and energy that it continues to generate "has been like a beautiful puzzle where every piece slots perfectly into place from conception through to its completion and beyond."

"This project was basically a succession of magical moments."

'Petite Mort (Parfum d'une Femme)'
by Marc Atlan

Composite 1510 by Fileti © 2011.
'Maiden's Belt' by Strumpet & Pink

FULFILLING DESIRE

It is here we merge with the voluptuousness of desire
and redolence, blending in ripe-ness, fecundity and
a light lick of lunacy. Filling and spilling, the pace is
untempered, colors lay on texture while thoughts and
ideas overlay and superimpose. Colours with temperature are found here and pay homage to the intensity
of feeling. We no longer contemplate desire for we
are surrendered in the visceral atmosphere amidst the
tone of sensorial declaration.

We cannot completely 'think' or intellectualize about
fulfilling desire for we perceive it on an emotional
level, rather we must move into the body and journey
into the inside of it. The mouth, therefore, becomes
the flowered opening, the succulent orifice, a conduit
of delight through which pleasure and experience
can enter. We open our mouths, take in, and capture,
flavors fullness. These tactile adventures in sticky-
ness facilitate the passage from the outside into our
insides; where self and other are at play with desire's
aesthetically uneven surface. Exploring textures,
flavors, colors and forms, we relish in the pleasures
of the mouth as we acknowledge and feed our sense
intelligence; savouring the darkest chocolate, delighting
in the naughty quiver of jelly on the tongue or feeling

the tight eruptive burst of pink red juice from the
pomegranate seed. We allow the experience in.

Sense pleasure is a fundamental aspect to being human,
it is the nature of bodily perception, and the desire
to give and receive pleasure is a vital aspect of life
in the context of a greater whole. In appreciating
the small-scale actions, the momentary rituals and
delicate definitions of enjoyment, we tend to desires
budding blossom and consent to our emotional and
sensuous well-being.

In fulfilling desire our experience becomes whole, there
are no distinctions between inner and outer for it has
merged and blurred with pleasure and complexity,
a harmonious chaos, amidst the viscous. Mind and
body, heart and soul, fuse in the erotic embrace and
without terms or conditions. Non-linear and disor-
derly, we open and yield to abandonment. These are
our uncharted waters. And it is here where we find
our true selves.

Within the Fulfilling of desire we enter into the Cabinet
of Desire; a small, immersive volume, in which to
ponder and imagine. Nine artists have been invited to
contribute a stand-alone text piece. Thoughts, musings, wonderings; desire as written word. The Cabinet
is without parameters. You are invited to submerge
yourself in these writings. Let the imagination linger
for this is the fertile ground of desire.

"for it was not knowledge but unity that she desired, not inscriptions on tablets, nothing that could be written in any language known to men, but intimacy itself, which is knowledge"
—Virginia Woolf, To the Lighthouse

Chocolate Waterfall' (detail) by Bompas & Parr

'Wild Strawberries, Campari and Gin
Jelly' by Bompas & Parr

Opposite page: 'Chocolate Waterfall'
by Bompas & Parr 2011. "Bompas
& Parr built a five tonne Chocolate
Waterfall in London pulling together
their favorite beans from around the
world to create their first house blend.

Visitors donned a protective suit before
visiting a chocolate waterfall flowing
at a rate of 12,000 litres per hour before
bottling their own chocolate elixir to
take away."

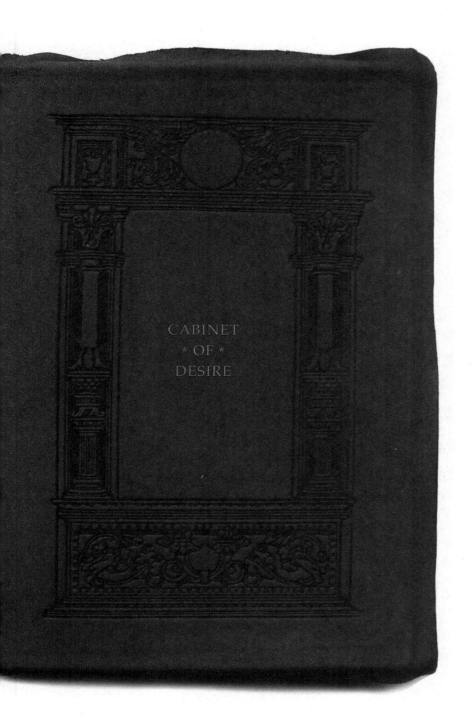

CABINET
* OF *
DESIRE

"Dawn was breaking over the river."—Chap. I., Book VI.

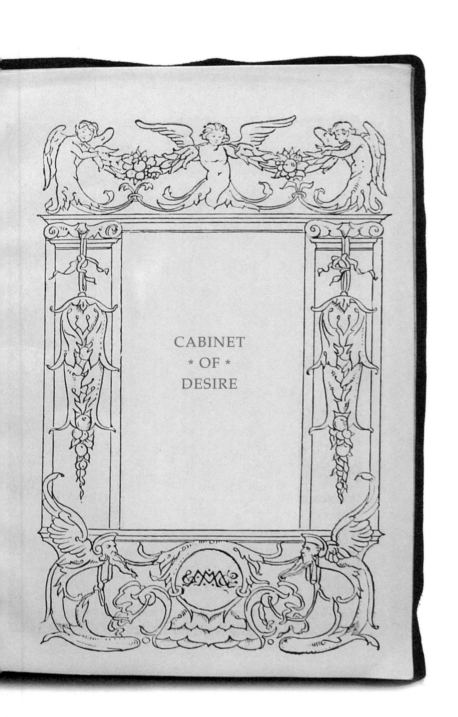

CABINET
* OF *
DESIRE

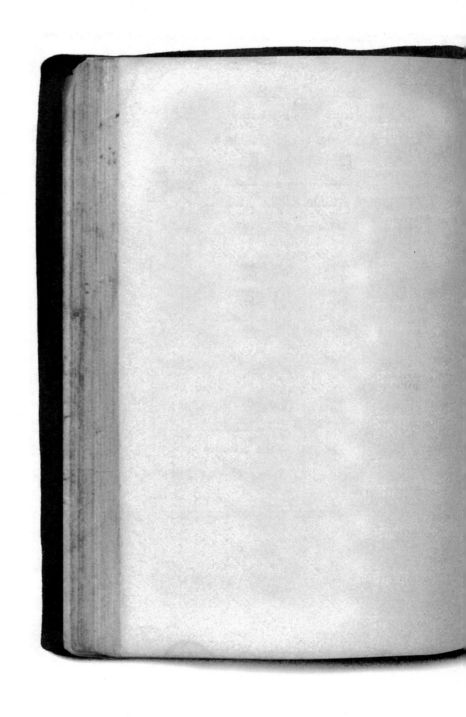

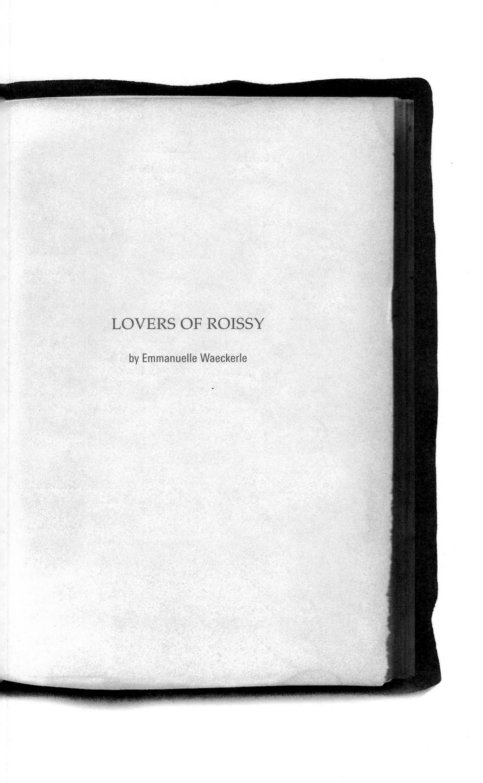

LOVERS OF ROISSY

by Emmanuelle Waeckerle

I

⟨ *Lovers of Roissy*

⟨ lover one ⟨ ⟨ O for ⟨
of
Montsouris
⟨ Monceau   together before   strolled   along
⟨ ⟨ ⟨   ⟨ down ⟨ ⟨ ⟨ on
                ⟨ ⟨ ⟨ ⟨ got ⟨ ⟨ ⟨
moved on towards ⟨ ⟨ of ⟨ ⟨ ⟨
⟨ two ⟨ ⟨ ⟨ ⟨ ⟨ ⟨ to
⟨ ⟨   ⟨ ⟨ corner ⟨
looks   for ⟨ does ⟨
⟨ ⟨ ⟨ ⟨ ⟨ ⟨ ⟨ ⟨ afternoon ⟨
⟨ ⟨ ⟨   ⟨
                        ⟨ blouse
no ⟨   on long gloves ⟨ ⟨ to
⟨ ⟨ of ⟨
⟨ got ⟨ ⟨   compact
⟨ ⟨ ⟨ off ⟨ slowly nor ⟨

9

—— to —— word to —— on
—— on —— down —— window
—— one —— too ——
—— to —— or so to ——
—— off —— gloves —— ——
your —— your —— to ——
—— beyond —— —— You too
—— clothing on —— your stockings roll
—— down to —— above your —— Go ——
—— some —— to hold —— stockings
—— —— not —— —— going
—— now —— doesn't —— to ——
turn around —— —— anyhow, ——
—— uncomfortable —— contact of
of —— upon —— ——
—— —— —— loosely ——
forth across —— 'Undo your ——
—— off your —— nothing to
—— —— to do —— hook ——
—— —— —— from
—— —— opens ——
—— —— 'You're not to
on your —— or on your ——
—— on —— without ——
—— covering —— sort of ——
—— —— sensation —— ——
—— to —— —— Now —— your
gloves —— on —— goes —— along ——
doesn't —— —— so —— so —— or

10

———————————— to ⟵ so motionless ⟶

so ⟵ so ———— so offered though so

thoroughly gloved ———⟶ going ———⟶

———— ————⟶ told — to do

————⟶or not to do ⟶ doesn't ————⟶

cross ⟶ or ———— together One

on ⟶ one on —— ———⟶ gloved

⟶ on ⟶ down

⟶ of ————⟶ ————⟶

⟵ ⟶ comes to ⟵ stop on ————

those ————⟶front of

———— mansion, you could ———— ————⟶

———— courtyard ———— ————

Faubourg ———⟶ mansions

no ———— ———— ————⟶

outside ———⟶ Don't move ⟶

'Don't move ———⟶

towards —— of ———⟶ ———⟶ ribbon

⟶ ⟶ unbuttons ⟶ buttons ⟶

———— forward ⟵ so ———⟶ ⟶about

to ———⟶ no ⟶got ———⟶

———— ⟶ only groping for ————

⟵ of ———⟶ ———⟶ ———— removes

———— ———⟶closed

now ———— ———— ———⟶

———— ———— ———⟶ ⟶ ———⟶

of ⟵ from ⟶ ————

———⟶ You

⟵ you You⟵ going to ⟵ out ⟵ go to ⟵

door ——————————— Someone — open —
door, whoever — you'll do —————You'll do
——————— of your own accord —
———————— you   you don't obey   once —
— you obey — No, you don't — your
———— more You don't ———— you're
——— whore ———— who's ———— you
————————————— Now go

Another version of ————— ——————
———— more ——— ——————young
woman ——— off ——— lover —
— second ———unknown — of —
——— drove — lover ——— —————
young woman ——— one who ————
—————— unknown ——— in front —
———— to — young woman ——— lover's —
—to ——————— now going to —
———————————— stockings
roll — down remove —————
——————— blindfold ———
———— would ——— to ————
———— would — instructions
course ————— so —
— once ———— bound ————
— about a ———————
— out of ————————
blindfolded ——— one or two doors —
— found — alone — blindfold gone

12

———————————————room —————
for ———— hour for ———— for two —— don't
know ——————————— though ——————————
——— door ——— opened ——————————————
——— on you could ——————————————————
——— room ——— room comfortable ——— odd
——————————————— on ——— floor ———— not
——— of ——————————— room ——————————
——————————— with cupboards Two ——— opened
——— door ——— two ——— young women costumed
————————————————————————————————— long
——————————————— to ——————————
bodices ——————————— ————————————————
——————— or hooked ———————— ————————
——————— elbow ————————gloves to
———— ————————— mouths ———— ——————————
wore collar around ———— ———— ———— on

——————— know ———— ————— O's ———
——— point ——————————————————— told
——— to ——— ————— going to ——————————
——————————————————————————————— ———
——— —————— for —————— ——————————
——— clothes ——————— ———— one of ——— cupboards
——————— not ——— do ——— own ——————————

——————————— would ————— ——————— ——— one of
those——— ——————— ——————— ———your ———
is——— ——————— ———— come ——— ———
13

I WANT

by Giorgio Sadotti

_

I WANT

I WANT YOU

I WANT YOU TO

I WANT YOU TO BE

I WANT YOU TO BE WHAT

I WANT YOU TO BE WHAT I

I WANT YOU TO BE WHAT I WANT

I WANT YOU TO BE WHAT I WANT YOU

I WANT YOU TO BE WHAT I WANT YOU TO

I WANT YOU TO BE WHAT I WANT YOU TO BE

I WANT YOU TO BE WHAT I WANT YOU TO

I WANT YOU TO BE WHAT I WANT YOU

I WANT YOU TO BE WHAT I WANT

I WANT YOU TO BE WHAT I

I WANT YOU TO BE WHAT

I WANT YOU TO BE

I WANT YOU TO

I WANT YOU

I WANT

_

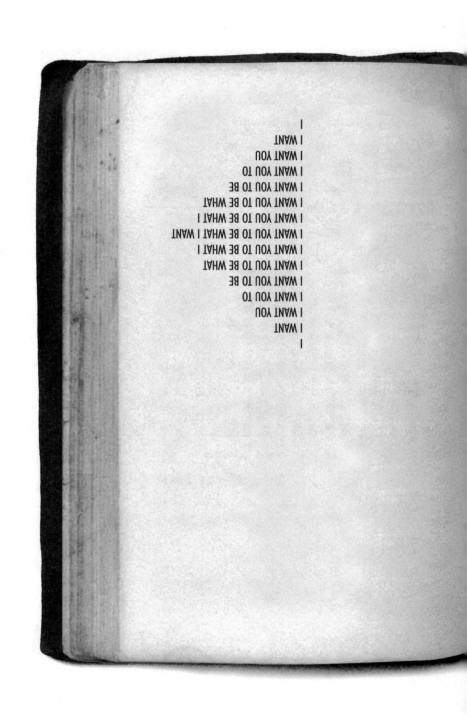

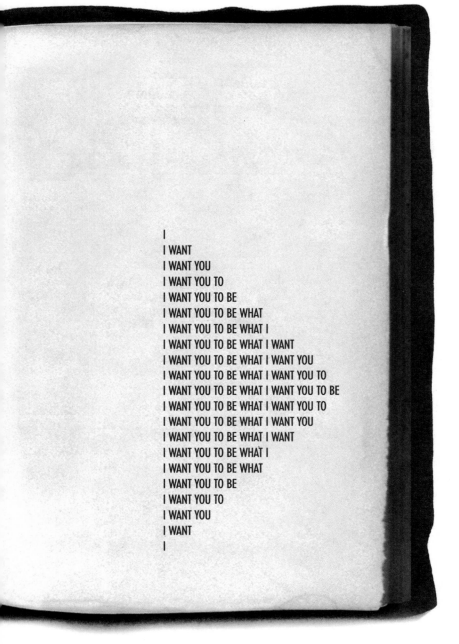

I
I WANT
I WANT YOU
I WANT YOU TO
I WANT YOU TO BE
I WANT YOU TO BE WHAT
I WANT YOU TO BE WHAT I
I WANT YOU TO BE WHAT I WANT
I WANT YOU TO BE WHAT I WANT YOU
I WANT YOU TO BE WHAT I WANT YOU TO
I WANT YOU TO BE WHAT I WANT YOU TO BE
I WANT YOU TO BE WHAT I WANT YOU TO
I WANT YOU TO BE WHAT I WANT YOU
I WANT YOU TO BE WHAT I WANT
I WANT YOU TO BE WHAT I
I WANT YOU TO BE WHAT
I WANT YOU TO BE
I WANT YOU TO
I WANT YOU
I WANT
I

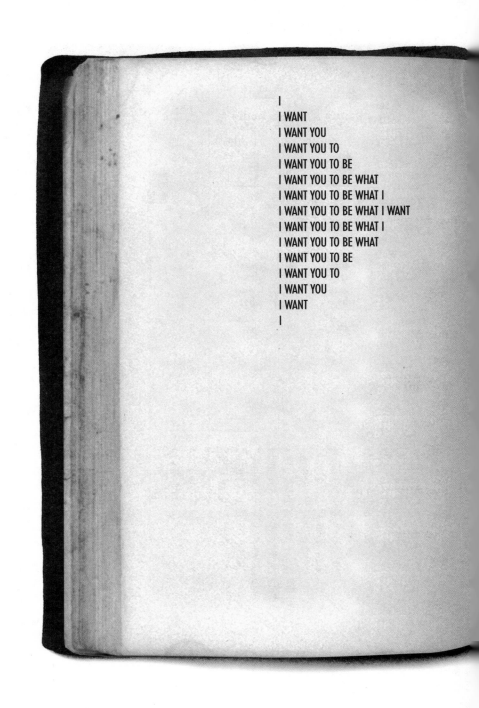

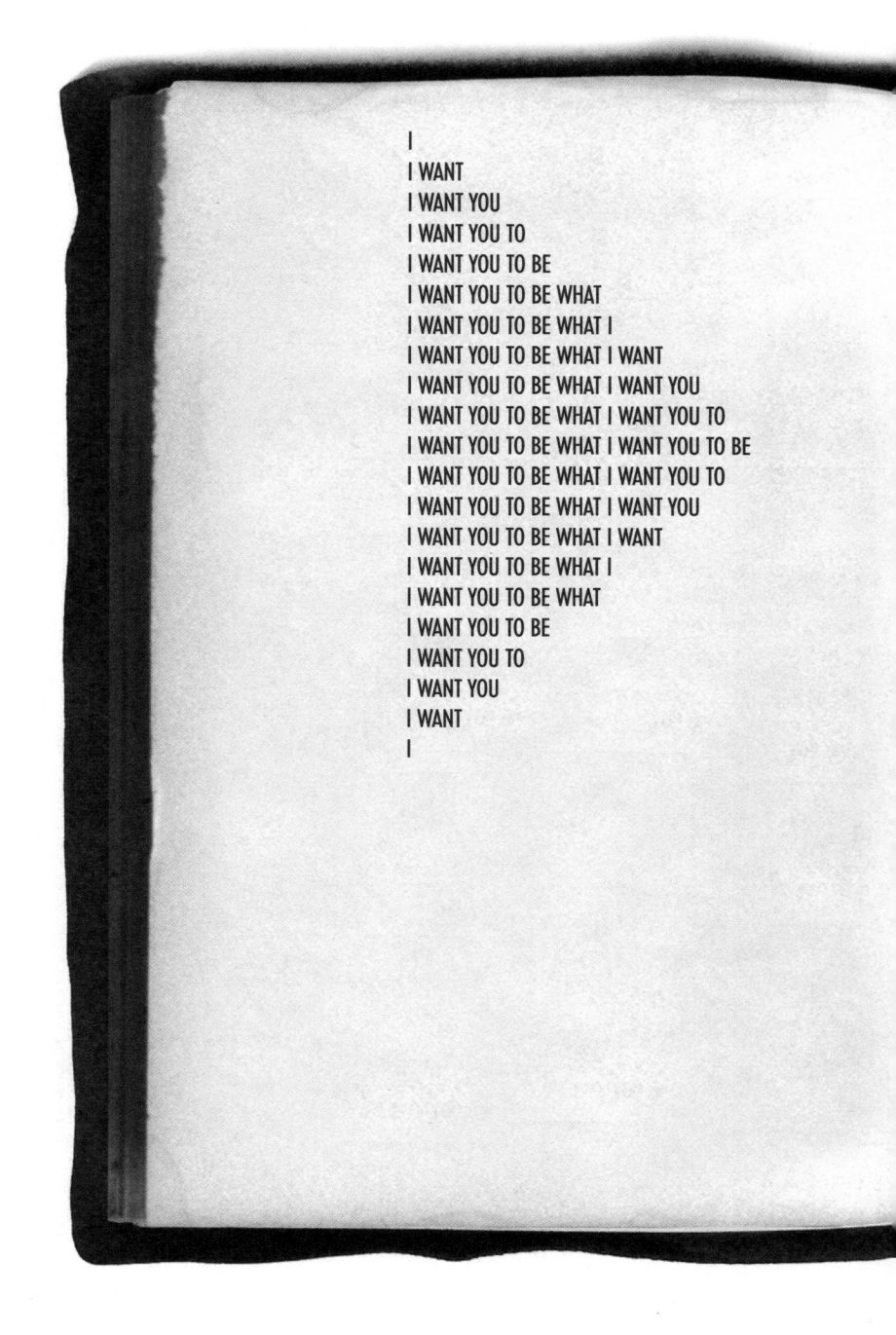

I
I WANT
I WANT YOU
I WANT YOU TO
I WANT YOU TO BE
I WANT YOU TO BE WHAT
I WANT YOU TO BE WHAT I
I WANT YOU TO BE WHAT I WANT
I WANT YOU TO BE WHAT I WANT YOU
I WANT YOU TO BE WHAT I WANT YOU TO
I WANT YOU TO BE WHAT I WANT YOU TO BE
I WANT YOU TO BE WHAT I WANT YOU TO
I WANT YOU TO BE WHAT I WANT YOU
I WANT YOU TO BE WHAT I WANT
I WANT YOU TO BE WHAT I
I WANT YOU TO BE WHAT
I WANT YOU TO BE
I WANT YOU TO
I WANT YOU
I WANT
I

IN THE GARDEN OF EARTHLY DELIGHTS

by Jane Wildgoose

Noon in the garden. The hottest day of the year, though it is late summer, almost autumn. The sun hammers down on her nakedness. Sweat slides between her breasts. A musky smell hangs in the air; her nose twitches involuntarily as she draws her face close to the sheen of that taut, tight skin.

He slithers rapidly though almost imperceptibly closer in the long grass. "Touch it" he whispers, urgently, almost hisses.

"Father said he'd kill me if I ever did…" she recoils. Slightly.

"Huh. Father. What does he know?" He hangs over her, his tongue flickering rapidly in and out over her wet skin.

The sun shifts imperceptibly closer. Not a cloud in the sky. The garden is parched and dry, aching for rain. The heat is unbearable, intense, unavoidable. Not a murmur of breath anywhere except for the two of them there in the long grass. No stirring in the branches of the fig tree, not a movement in the cedar, only the outpouring of scents: the late roses, drooping under the weight of their heavy petals, red and white; their perfume oversweet, verging on rank.

She hesitates. Frowns slightly; wrinkles her nose.
Focuses again on that taut skin and the musky smell.

"Go on, touch it." A whisper that is almost a hiss.

Hesitatingly, she moves her hand.

Hesitatingly, she touches that taut, tight skin.

He moves involuntarily, imperceptibly, then swiftly –
is it he who jerks her head? Does she make this rapid
movement of her own accord? Her lips envelop him
as if he is ripe fruit, and in an immediate reciprocal
movement, he is down there in amongst the lilies.

Meanwhile - as if out of nowhere - a tiny cloud is
sneaking up on the sun. The garden gradually darkens,
but the two of them – how would they notice at a moment like this?

Time passes…they are lost to the garden.

By the time the clouds have fully gathered they are
sleeping.

It is afternoon, but it seems like midnight, and winter,
here in the garden.

They wake, abruptly, as the storm takes hold. It is completely black overhead and the garden is lost to them.

Shivering and terrified, Adam and Eve scramble to their feet, gaze deep into one another's eyes - but in the dark, seeing only a stranger, frantically cover their nakedness with shame and ragged fig leaves.

Out of the garden they are expelled to a new life, with a certain end.

Meanwhile the snake slithers away, imperceptibly, his forked tongue flickering rapidly in and out over the flattened wet grass.

The ants gather and teem on the discarded apple core with its hard bright seeds gleaming against the dank earth.

THE LAST BOUDOIR OF
MARIE ANTOINETTE

by Ed Hollis

On the 5th October 1789, in the afternoon, a man enters a clearing in an enchanted forest. He rides up to the door of a little house; but he may not see the enchantress who lives there, the servants tell him: she has gone inside, because it is raining.

'Then beg her to come at once.' he tells them; and they go inside to find her: up the stone stairs, through the antechamber, the dining room, and the salon de compaignie, to the bedchamber.

It is with some trepidation that the servants knock on the last door, for on the other side of it is the room that everyone has been talking about. The boudoir is studded with rubies, they say, and even the paint that covers the walls, in subtle shades of grey, suffused with green, violet, or pink, is perfumed with, herbs, with lavender, and roses.

And this is the room, they say, in which L'Autrichienne (the Austrian bitch) as they call her, pursues her amours – with men, women, children, dildoes, anyone and anything who will do it with her:

> *In a fine alcove artfully gilded,*
> *Not too dark and not too light,*
> *On a soft sofa, covered in velvet,*
> *The August Beauty bestows her charms*
> *[and] the Prince presents the Goddess his cock…*

They say she watches herself in the mirrors that line
every wall, the shameless protagonist and the titillated
audience in her own filthy performance.

But when the door opens, there are no rubies, and
no mirrors. The walls are panelled in virginal blue
and white. The fireplace is square and simple, and
the furniture is upholstered in silk of the palest grey.

A woman is sewing. Her large nose, and bulbous,
watery eyes are matronly. She does not look like
an enchantress. The servants pass on the message,
and the woman stands up, and puts down her
sewing, and leaves her infamous boudoir for the
last time.

It is the last room that will ever protect or pleasure her.

Once she is gone, taken outside in her underwear, and
guillotined in the middle of Paris, there is nothing to
stop anyone from entering the last boudoir of Marie
Antoinette. The locks of gilded bronze have been stolen,
and the windows smashed. Inside, the furniture has
been sold or broken, and the canvasses ripped down
from the walls. Everyone is disappointed by what they
find: the room is not what they had imagined it to be.

Or it does not seem so at first: it takes the Revolutionaries a while to work out the secret of the boudoir: it
is revealed by pressing a button on the wall. Nothing

happens, since the servants fled the moment their mistress left the room; but when the revolutionaries track them down, they tell them what used to happen. It goes something like this:

Slowly, smoothly, panels rose out of the floor. Within a minute or so, the view of the gardens was replaced with mirrors, and, in the sparkling gloom, all Marie Antoinette could see is herself.

The Queen's button activated a bell, you see, and the bell activated the servants hidden in the basement, and they turned the cranks to make the mirrors slide noiselessly up through the floor upstairs.

The boudoir was just what they'd thought it was all along: a secret, monstrous machine, powered not by magic, but by functionaries whose forgotten lives were devoted to one purpose alone – their own invisibility.

Marie Antoinette was an enchantress; and her boudoir, while she pouted in it, was a spectacle constructed for the enjoyment of one person. It was a magic mirror that showed its owner her hearts desire; and, most monstrously, all the Queen saw there was herself.

Now we can all look into the magic mirrors, and, after repeated restoration, they are raised and lowered by electricity. Marie Antoinette has become a cult, and her boudoir a shrine; but it has been violated by the common gaze and the ordinary light of day. Like all desire, it is a secret moment in time that has been lost.

BE/LONGING

by Silvia Ziranek

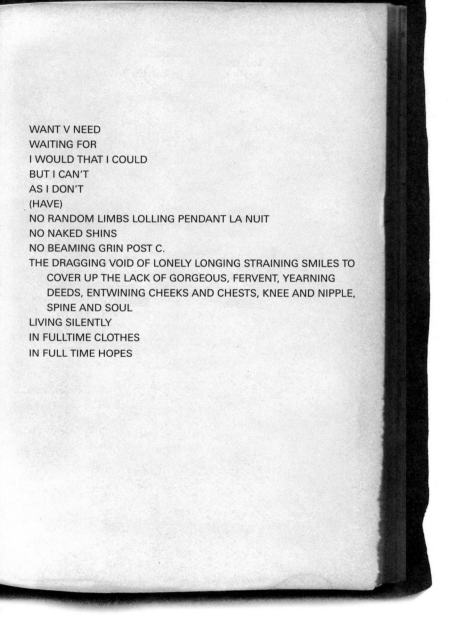

WANT V NEED
WAITING FOR
I WOULD THAT I COULD
BUT I CAN'T
AS I DON'T
(HAVE)
NO RANDOM LIMBS LOLLING PENDANT LA NUIT
NO NAKED SHINS
NO BEAMING GRIN POST C.
THE DRAGGING VOID OF LONELY LONGING STRAINING SMILES TO
    COVER UP THE LACK OF GORGEOUS, FERVENT, YEARNING
    DEEDS, ENTWINING CHEEKS AND CHESTS, KNEE AND NIPPLE,
    SPINE AND SOUL
LIVING SILENTLY
IN FULLTIME CLOTHES
IN FULL TIME HOPES

AN ENCYCLOPEDIA OF DESIRE

by. Michael Petry

D

dumb, dense, DEADLY, delightful, delicious, **dribbling**, **dilated**, *dildoed*, **disturbed**, *dishy*, distrustful, *delirious*, **DILTF**, dirty, dirtier, *dirtiest*, dick, *dicked*, doctored, *deterrent*, **deviance**, **defiance**, *devastating*, devastation, devastate, detonate, **dethroning**, **demanding**, denying, distortionate, **detour**, DISTURBING, *distrustful*, *distressing*, *distracted*, **demonic**, daily, dalliance, damaging, DAMASCENE, **driven**, damnable, *draconian*, DRAMATIC, *draped*, DRAWN, **drifting**, dressed, disrobed, **doggy-style**, *drained*, drilled, **drunk**, dangled, *dappled*, distraught, dark, darker, darkest

E

eyes, eggs, ears, **edifice**, *edifying*,
erogenous, **EXTRUDED**, **embryonic**,
embroidered, **embrace**, *embracing*,
EMBRACED, ENDED, encompassing,
enchained, **EMBOLDENED**,
encoded, *encompassed*, **ENCOMPASSING**,
enclothed, **encircled**, enchanted, *ebullient*,
exasperating, **exasperated**, **EXTREME**,
EXTRUDED, eager, **extravagant**,
extravagantly extramural, ENLACED,
extraordinary, extraordinarily enchanting,
engorged, engrossed, **enhanced**,
enigmatic, enlarged, **enlargement**, ease,
easy, easy, EASY, edible, *eat*,
EATEN, **EDGY**, eerie, **EDUCATIVE**,
effective, **effect**, EFFORTLESS

S

simple, **sexual**, single, singled, *sexy*,
spunky, *shove*, **shoved**, SHOWERED,
showering, showered, showy, shrill,
shuddering, shunted, *sizzling*,
sketchy, skew, skiff, **skin**, *skinned*,
slavering, *slabber*, slobber, *saliva*,
slam, **slammed**, SPANK, *spunked*,
sparkle, *spasm*, **spasmodic**, spasmodically,
SHIMMERING, shimmy, saddled, salacious,
salient, SAPPHIC, satyriasis, **saucy**,
scarring, **SCATTERED**, seam,
SECRETIONS, *seditious*, SEDUCTIVE,
SEDUCTION, *seed*, **seeded**, SEEDY,
seminal, shaving, ***shaved***,
SHATTERED, sheer, SHIVER, shivering,
shoot, *shot*, **SPENT**

I

insidious, indispensable, initial, **initiate**,
inflate, **inflated**, **inflatable**, *inside*,
itchy, ignited, igniting, *ignitable*,
INGLORIOUS IGNITER, ignoble,
irritating, *issuance*, irresistible,
irremovable, **IRREVERENT**, **irremediable**,
irreducible, irreconcilable, *impartial*,
impacted, **impactive**, impacting, *icarian*,
iconic, ideal, idyllic, *inelegant*,
illuminating, **illuminate**, illuminator,
illusory, IRONIC, irrational,
irreclaimable, *imaginative*, immolate,
immolation, immolator, *immortal*, **imminent**,
immiscible, immediate, ***immediately***
IMMOLATED, *inward*, intimacy,
irrealizable

R

rosebuds, **restless**, romps, restraint, restraints, **ramrods**, roses, rush, rushing, **resentment**, *rest*, rumble, **reverberate**, *run*, runny, relax, REAR, *rear-ended*, reð, **REDDER**, *remembrance*, rudeness, **ruddy**, *rugby*, *relax*, REIGN, **rein**, REGULATION, regulatory, regularity, **remarkable**, *relish*, *relishing*, remaining, RENT, repast, *REPAIR*, REPARING, *repaired*, REPLENISHED, repine, RAMPANT, **rake**, ram, RAGE, raunch, **raunchy**, randy, rank, **reckless**, reflective, round, **roundhead**, **rotund**, rubenesque, rub, rubbing rough, rubbery, *ruck*, *ruination*

E

EROS, *erotomania*, **eroticized**,
egocentric, egomania, egomaniacal,
ectoplasm, ENDLESS **excitement**,
effervescent, equipment, **equip**,
EFFICIENT, egalitarian, exonerated,
exonerating, *errant*, *eruption*, **erupting**,
erupted, **elephantine**, escheated, enslaved,
enslaving, *escorting*, escort, escorts,
essential, esteemed, episodic, ephebe,
ephemeral, *ephemerally* epicene,
epicurean, equivocal, equivocally
etherean, EUPHORIA, euphoric,
euphorically electric, ELEGIAC, *elegant*,
elevated, elevating, **ERECTING**, **ERECT**,
exact, *exacting*, ever, **ENLIGHTENING**,
enlightened

OH THAT FEELING

by Shine

I have thought lots about the dream of life, how it holds each of us in a different way.

It came to me as a four-year-old, an image of a great big pair of brown rubber boots, my own, reaching up to the sky, with strap and buckle across the top of the foot, known to all children who have worn rubber boots with shoes in them.

Maybe it started by putting my shoes in and out of them, that tight feeling, then snap and your feet appear/disappear to a nice little sound, maybe with an added flap against your calves as you stand up. Yikes!

If your feet are going into the boots, it is a different feel and sound from if they are coming out. Do you feel the difference? Do it in your mind. Going in, your heel pushes tightly against the stretchy inside calf of the boot. You pull the tops of the rubber, and plop—a good tight fit of feet into the boot. But when you let go of the tops, the smooth tubular rubber is left free to flap against your beautiful, muscular calves. Feel it! Plop, then wobble-snap, wobble-snap!

Coming out of the rubber boot is just as satisfying only much different. You pull the opposite end of the boot, the foot and heel, working it so the rubber tube wobbles back and forth against your calf. Suddenly it gives and you feel the satiny smooth rubber loose against your calf, as it slides off. Youch!

So, if that is the beginning, what is the middle and the end? There is much more to tell. Every sense gets added to the plot, in different ways, based upon different circumstances and different times of this dream of life. It wobbles right up into your brain. I could tell you anecdotes of when different senses held sway and why. I could go where Freud has gone and tell you that tubular rubber around the leg goes both ways, as female genitalia or male genitalia, dominant or submissive, humiliation or pride, flowing in and out like the metronomic wobble of rubber itself.

But the childhood dream of life, that first glimpse, the simplicity of moving into and out of pliable, smooth, sensuous, rubbery material, the snap, pop, the vacuum, the extraterrestrial smell, the stares of attention, the wide open sky. Does this sentence need an ending?

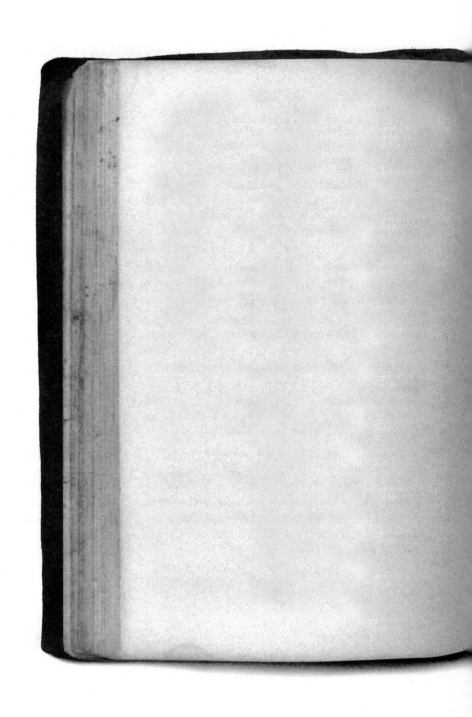

STRAIGHT JACKET

by Eric Magnuson

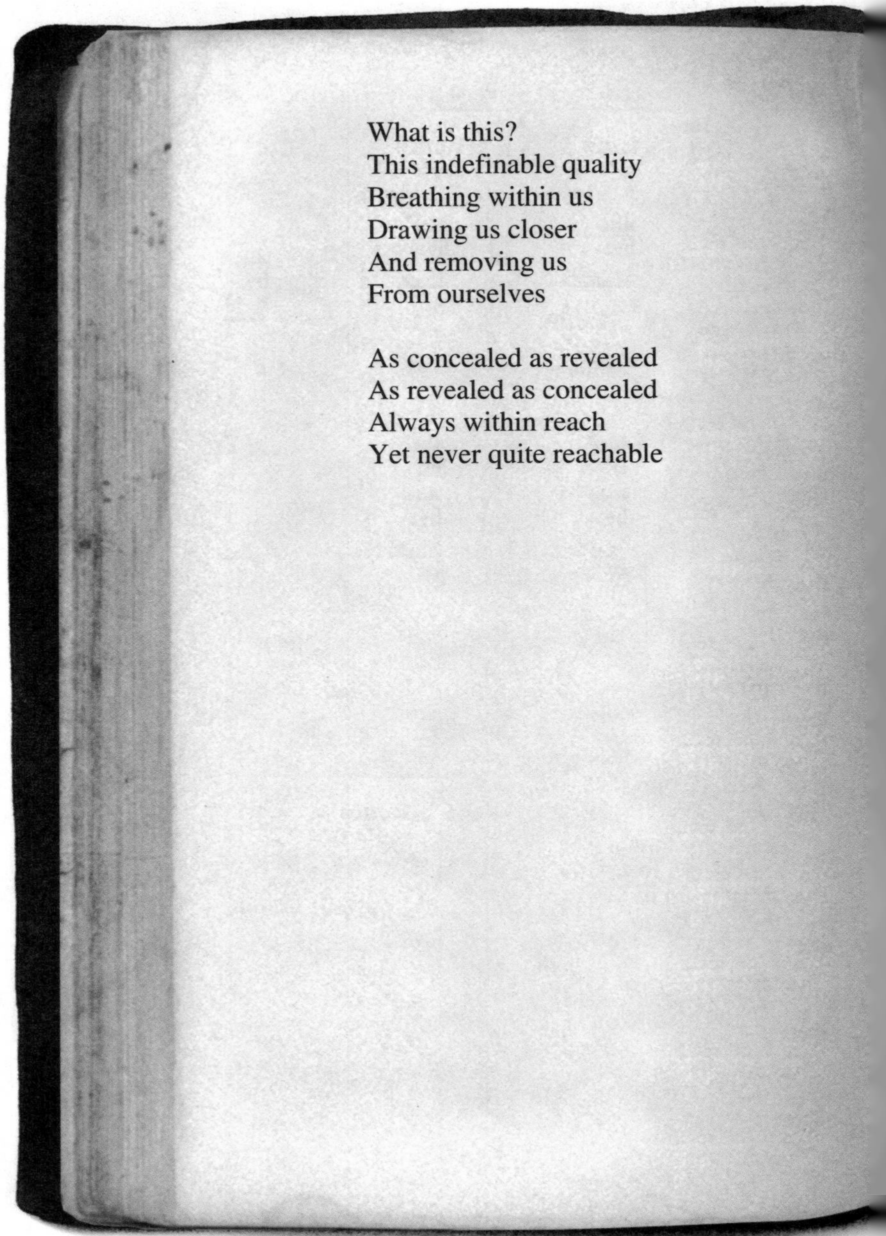

What is this?
This indefinable quality
Breathing within us
Drawing us closer
And removing us
From ourselves

As concealed as revealed
As revealed as concealed
Always within reach
Yet never quite reachable

Dearest object of desire
Beseeched within pleading
Required and appealed
So very sweetly appealing

With lips whispered sealed
Yearning in this petition
Silent darling listening
Secret hushed expression

Wishing pleaded wanting
A flavor resisting tasting
Craving licking longing
Conjured in solicitation

Stripped of every meaning
Mirrored in our reflection
Considered and resisting
Depriving as possession

Shadowed in plain sight
Patterned to perception
Deception as delight
Pure distilled obsession

An ideal in every given
Delayed and tantalized
Mislaid the very moment
You are truly realized

eam 2011

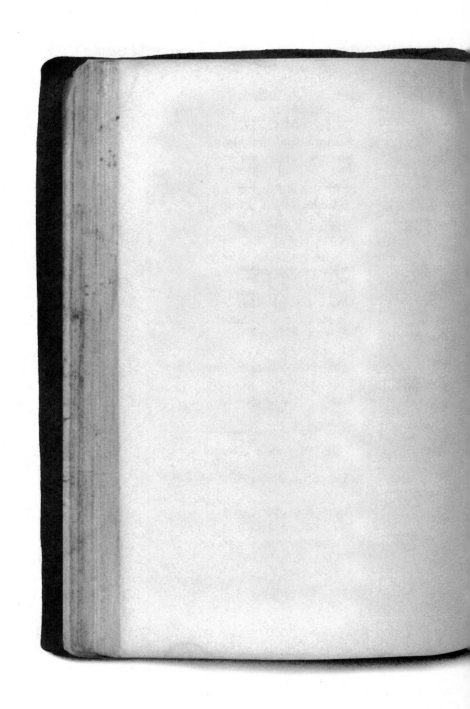

HER LORDSHIP'S AMUSEMENT

by Midori

She leaned back into the throne and leisurely cleaned her delicate paw. She had particularly delicate small paws, which among many other features, she found displayed her royal refinement and lineage. Her other paw rested firmly on the leash, though it really wasn't necessary, as her pet was now highly obedient – generally. But she enjoyed displaying her authority in private and public. Anyway, she knew these creatures, being pack-oriented by nature, required constant reminder of their place and authority of the Alpha. Owners who mistook sloppy sentimentality for good pet keeping inevitably found destroyed furniture and revolts on their paws.

She rang for her attendant, who swiftly entered through the floor door. Graceful as ever, the attendant's well kept multi colored fur shimmered in the golden shafts of afternoon light falling through the window. Perceiving Her Lordship's instructions, she continued the full post-slumber grooming, paying particular attention to the paper-thin ears and the space between them on the crown. Her Lordship's closed her eyes and deep purring emitted from somewhere deep in her noble chest.

Pet watched silently. Both the women read envy in his face, but as ever they were not sure, as these creatures neither sent or received communication without vocalization. They often wondered and speculated on the range of emotional and thoughts these species were capable of. Some researchers found that they were able to engage in rudimentary telepathy with neural augmentation and considerable training over decades, but these studies were still in their early stages.

If Pet envied her personal attendant's grooming privileges, he could just suffer in his envy, she thought. Her Lordship wasn't about to be cleaned with his limp wet sponge of a tongue. He could keep his vulgar tongue licking to females of his species at the breeding yard.

With a twitch of a whisker she dismissed her attendant, who backed away and slipped silently down the floor door, leaving them alone.

Pet sat up eagerly in anticipation. Stretching herself out languorously on her side, she tugged at the jewel-laden leash. Pet stood up, fully naked, except the ornate gold filament collar around his neck that the leash attached to. After so many years, she still marveled at their furless nakedness. Initially they seemed so ugly to her, with flesh wrinkles and odd tufts of wiry fur in scattered places. She first acquired them for her vanity menagerie, but eventually she grew genuinely fond of them and her collection grew rapidly. Now she ranked as one of the territory's best breeders and trainers of the species.

His genitals stirred as he stood before her. The flaccid bit of barbless flesh swelled and rose to salute her as he stood in impeccable attention waiting for the few simple commands she taught him. He was not the smartest of his kind, but he was exceptionally beautiful and more loyal and eager than any of her previous stock. She looked forward to siring his line for these particular traits and marketing his stud services. He truly had Imperial-Crown potential.

She nodded her head towards the cabinets and let the leash slack. With hands behind his back, he followed his erection towards the cabinet. The leash reached its limit and went taught just as he reached the door. Straining against his collar, he pressed on the cabinet door, which slid open noiselessly to reveal a woven golden basket. Face turning red from the tightening collar, he grabbed it and stepped back swiftly to catch his breath. She tugged impatiently at his leash. Pet obediently trotted back to stand at the base of the lush padded platform that was her throne.

One delicate paw extended leisurely towards him. Amber and silver bands of soft fur alternated up her limb. With deliberate ease she stretched her digits and held out the razor sharp claws before his eyes. He stood frozen. She nodded towards the basket in his arms. Hastily he opened the lid and extracted several diminutive curved sheaths of gold, jewel encrusted and ending in a bulbous gold tip. One by one, he deftly slid the custom claw covers onto each deadly claw. Lined in cork and gold velvet, the claws sank satisfyingly into them. When he finished all four digits of the first paw, she extended the other towards him. She did not have him cover her hind paws as she was in a slow sweet mood. No need for the rambunctious disemboweling kicks tonight.

As he was about to cover her last front claw, she retracted it. He froze, with one hand holding out the sheath between his thumb and forefinger. His cock bobbed as he swallowed hard.

She whipped the bare claw out and pressed its needle sharp tip to his chest. His breathing grew shallow, trying to keep his chest from moving too deeply.

Her whiskers and ears perked towards him. The slits of her eyes dilated, blackness filling the emerald green field. The edges of her mouth curled up as her cheeks puffed up.

She pierced the skin and savoured his wincing. He bit his lip and kept his silence.

The tip of her extended tail twitched.
He braced himself.

Her eyes narrowed and whiskers reached further towards him, touching and sensing his face, taking in his imperceptible quivers.

He let out a wail and dropped the basket as she slashed swiftly down his chest. He still held the last claw cover aloft.

Good Pet, she thought – but sadly he could not perceive her compliment.

Blood flowed from wound. Their skins were so thin and delicate, she mused, it's a wonder their species survived before ownership. Her cutting was precise and controlled. Her skill in toying with this kind, without harm or fatality, also made her legendary among the collectors and enthusiasts.

She extended the bloody bare claw to him. Gasping still from the blow, he carefully slid the last sheath on her. She sunk the tip satisfyingly into the silk and cork lining. Leaning on her elbows she leaned into his bleeding chest and sniffed the sweet smell of obedient prey. She licked the blood and wound with fully extended tongue. He flinched as the barbed tongue raked across the slash. The saliva burned hot in his cut. Soon the wound would bubble and swell, but then heal remarkably faster for her ministrations. The healing properties of her people's saliva on their flesh were not only legendary, but also scientifically proven.

She was, after all, a kind and loving owner.

It took a few moments but his breathing finally began to slow.

Then she nodded again, this time to the back of the throne. He trotted over and fetched an elegant onyx vessel with a long fluted neck. He returned to his post at her throne and awaited command.

She rolled back onto her back and stretched out all her limbs. Her gaze never left him even as she rolled around languorously. The amber rosettes of her flank disappeared as she exposed her delicate silver chest and belly to him. She extended and spread her thighs invitingly.

He raised the vessel up high and poured the viscous oil-like silver liquor onto his rigid and smooth cock. He moved the stream up to his chest dramatically splashed the last burst onto his chest. With furless fingers he rubbed the liquor over his chest, down his stomach, coated his hairless testicles and finally grasped his throbbing shaft. He stroked his thick cock for her in full obedient display. He was large even for his species, and certainly larger than any of the Toms in this territory, barbs included. His body glowed in silver glory and wafted of intoxicating scent.

She hadn't allowed him release or stud service in recent weeks, so he was particularly demonstrative. She did not dress his cock with the barbed sheath tonight, so he he'd be allowed direct stimulation. He likely hoped to come if she let him.

If he could purr, she thought, he'd be purring louder than the proudest Toms around, but alas, he could not purr.

She signaled him to mount the throne and stand over her. He obeyed swiftly, stroking his baton without missing a beat. He stood straddling her. He began to moan. She whipped her tail twice disapprovingly against the platform. He snapped his hands back behind him and stood at attention. His cock bobbed begging for attention.

Sitting up on her elbows, she brought her face to his strange dancing thickness and wrinkled, throbbing testicles. Her cheeks puffed and whiskers jerked towards him, tickling his smooth thighs.

She extended her barbed, bone-cleaning tongue and held it at the base of his shaft. He looked down and gasped a tiny explosion of terror at the realization of her intent.

Perhaps he wasn't so dumb after all, she thought.

She always wondered if they could come from her tongue alone.

'Jaba Couch' by Mark Brazier-Jones.
Silver plated bronze castings.
Photographed in situ at The Vyne, the
former stately home of Sir John Chute

Opposite page: 'An Indian Jellyscape'
for Tata Naka's S/S 2011 runway by
Bompas & Parr

Opposite page: The Lake & Stars F/W
2010 Campaign

'Bandi Console' (detail) by Mark
Brazier-Jones

INTERVIEW WITH MARK BRAZIER-JONES

First Object of Desire: The Captain Scarlet Spectrum Pursuit Vehicle.

The tone was set at a tender age for Mark Brazier-Jones, whose attraction to the Captain Scarlet Pursuit Vehicle matured into a passion for motorbikes and machine orien-tated, masculine 'projectile' objects. He personifies his theory regarding men and boys and their objects of desire. That is, they are inextricably drawn to anything with "projecting power," in essence, he says, "like an ejaculation;" bows and arrows, spears, guns, motorcycles and cars. He believes, unquestionably, in the differentiation between that which a man desires and the desires of a woman. However, where he does differ considerably, is in his creativity where he uni-fies these distinctions. His motivation and mission, he states, "is to please women absolutely" and he does this sublimely well. There is a masculine characteristic to his creations, returning to the 'projection of power' but combined with lusciously sensuous forms and seductive materials. Perhaps, then, this is why his pieces feel so very complete for they are a fusion between the duality of male and female. He is 'projecting' towards the female and she responds to the protuberance voluptuously.

There is a delicious juxtaposition, a blending, of esoteric meanings and symbols of power combined with decorative forms which take their queue from nature in the majority of his pieces; "An amalgam of thoughts and ideas that I play with over time." Textures, and more importantly the layering of texture, combined with materials linked to what he believes appeal to man's inquisitive nature and magpie- type fetish (i.e things that glint in the light), are consistently present in his furniture creations.

He sees an idea for a chair, a light, a chaise longue as fully formed, complete in his mind. The task of bringing this 'seen' object to life is ongoing until, quite literally, Mark recognizes the piece as being desirable. He senses this through the internal points of registration. A piece is finished, complete, "when it strikes a particular note; when the object is both familiar and yet absolutely new." This known and unknown characteristic could be considered a Surrealist agenda however Mark does not consider himself or his work to be Surrealist.

The Flashman series began about seven years ago and showed a distinct sexual and erotic departure to his previous more fluidly sensuous works. The motivation for this innovative body of work combined the opportunity to create a piece for the newly opened erotic boutique Coco de Mer, in London, with the revelation that the fastest growing industry was the sex industry. Mark decided "to get his finger in this very interesting pie."

His research into sexually specific furniture seemed to fall into two distinct, and rather repellent, categories. The first being "grizzly dungeon iron-smith type gear," the second being "sporty gymnasium equipment and neither of them would you want in any room that your Aunty might visit." Above all, they were so pre-meditated that it became un-sexy. The Flashman series landed in Mark's imagination, complete. "It explored and fitted the English sexual psyche, which was all about the notion of Victorian carryings-on in Hertfordshire with raucous parties" and, quite literally, "all the horsey 'tally-ho' goings on."

The first piece he created was the Poker Table, with five legs and taking the human form to be a five-pointed star. Mark heard some statistic regarding the office table or desk being the most common place for people to have sex. He measured the height of the desk and so the height of the Poker Table was decided. After this the other pieces in the series pretty much fell into line in his imagination straight away. "Tally-Ho," "The Shoe Shine Chair" and the "Study Chair."

All of the pieces do have this glorious quality that you somehow know them yet they are completely new. His aim was to cre-ate "the sort of pieces that looked as though they had been part of some Victorian folly; an antique that uncle Henry had collected on a trip to the Far East." The beauty lies in the provenance that Mark has instilled in each piece and as such his creations of highly sexual and technically adept pieces of 'furniture' can be dotted around the house without draw-ing too much attention. Although they are insanely unique there is also a level of subtlety to these pieces. They are fully formed, complete objects of desire within themselves and yet the genius comes from the fact that with one glance you inevitably begin to create a scenario of your own. "What if I were to...............on the Tally Ho?" This particular piece has been taken up most readily and has gained its own momen-tum over the years. From a trot, to a canter, it has now gal-loped off on its own journey of discovery and there are many who would relish the opportunity to ride along with it.

'Tally-ho' by Mark Brazier-Jones

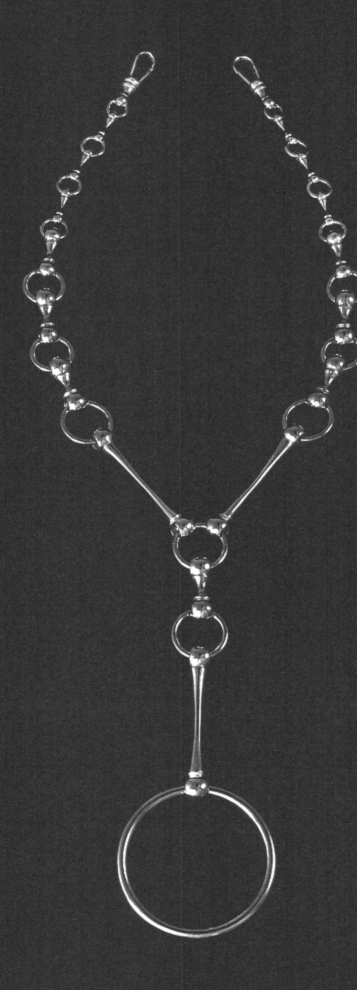

'Love Lock' by Betony Vernon. Sterling silver. *"The sexually empowering, equestrian inspired Love Lock is one of Betony's favourite jewels. The chain terminates with a silver shaft ring and sweetly binds, 'locks', lovers together. The provision of manual and oral pleasure takes on unexpected nuances for both partners."*

Opposite page: 'Anal Dilatation Kit' by Betony Vernon. Sterling silver

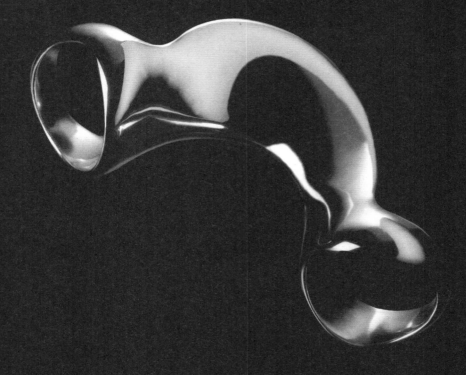

Top: 'Petting Ring'. Sterling silver
Bottom: 'The Shag Bague'. Sterling
silver

Opposite page: 'Soul-less Shoes'.
Sterling silver. All pieces by Betony
Vernon

NTERVIEW WITH BETONY VERNON

First accessory of desire: a fire-engine red leather shiny varnished waterproof coat.

First object of desire: a small footstool in the shape of a bull. As a young girl Betony Vernon would sit on the bull, grabbing hold of the ears and horns, and would rub herself against it. It was a play-thing but it also provided her with pleasure. These early body awakenings combined with a non-prohibitive upbringing created a fertile environment to nourish what and who she was to become; a ferociously intelligent, aware and passionate woman.

Betony Vernon began creating jewelry at the age of seventeen; developing and evolving her ideas into what she termed 'Wearable Temples'. Jewelry certainly is one of the number one objects of desire and is charged with all sorts of memories. "You charge it with your energies as it becomes part of your life. And yet it comes to you pre-charged with some sort of story from the person who created it. You, as the wearer then take this narrative, the story-line, you take it over and own it. It becomes yours - it's incredible – no?"

Designed over a period of 10 years, the 'Wearable Temples' collection consisted of about 1000 pieces and was incredibly successful. Betony's work was available in the most influential and key boutiques and stores around the world. In 1994 she began to develop a line of erotic pieces, which could be shared, dismantled and worn in various ways. The ideas were inspired by her sexual explorations and spiritual developments; Paradise Found. She was fully aware that these tangible erotic expressions were ahead of their time and therefore continued to expand her ideas for her own private use and for the occasional private collector.

September 11th shocked the world. The wreckage and trauma compelled Betony to shift her commercial focus. It was no longer enough for her to continue presenting her 'Wearable Temples.' "My desire to bring something beautiful into the world that centered around and encouraged people to love one another became the bridge to my mission - to empower men and women to obtain and provide greater degrees of sexual pleasure." She launched her Paradise Found collection, which up until that point had been hidden, and immediately lost all of her clients in the fashion world. Six months later she met Sam Roddick, the maverick who had just opened the radically different Coco de Mer in London. It was here that Betony found the first publically accessible home for her love inspired work and a different period of evolvement came into play. However, she also became acutely aware that for

her work to develop and progress, both creatively and as a designer, she was going to have to become a sexual educator; an integral part of her sensuous and sexual journey.

"One's sexual well-being is deeply connected to one's overall well being, we can't deny that. Freud believed that the fruit of all neurosis is sexual frustration and can lead to violence and contortion. I am not a big fan of Freudian psychology, but I concur with this view point."

Having used her body for her 'fieldwork' as she puts it, Betony has become acutely aware that the majority of people have no notion of the capacity of their pleasure. It is easy to 'spark' desire but, she questions, "How to increment that desire? How do I keep that desire alive?" It is a huge question, more so when the chemical shelf life of desire does indeed have a timer on it. "What do you do when the timer starts to tick? How do you make a twenty year relationship work? Being sexually literate combined with self-understanding and tolerance is a good foundation. Combined with a great deal of creativity both with your self and with your lover or lovers. We all know how we feel when spring is in the air but how can we have the spring throughout the year?" The energy does shift during these fertile months and the sap begins to rise. "The answer, you achieve springtime by paying attention to and nourishing your pleasure/s."

The difficulty today is that sex has become such a mechanical act, which is what we see on the internet, "a 'mechanical slamming' where the woman is still portrayed, for the most part, as an object of receptivity, omnipresent and giving and so often in positions which are not conducive to her orgasm." Not, as Betony says, that the orgasm is the only reason to make love, "but it is important that whatever sensations are generated does increase your sensitivity which will, ultimately, impact upon your final orgasm. Sometimes, of course, it is wonderful to simply 'give' your partner a particular position, for their pleasure. One of the biggest orgasm inhibitors is the misconception that partners have to please each other at the same time. It is an important part of pleasure to lay back and to be able to take it and not feel that you have to touch your partner at the same time. You can just accept and obtain it. Equally it is very important to be able to say, this is the position that will make me come, and come and come again – help me to do it." Many men are not actually ready for this and they wrongfully believe that a woman's pleasure is similar to that of a man's. But equally, through a lack in personal knowledge and understanding, many women have also masculinized their own pleasure, believing that one orgasm is

Portrait of Betony Vernon
by Ali Mahdavi

enough or that 'one' is all they can have." Betony responds with a resounding "No! With one orgasm you are just at the very beginning of something transcendental and a 30 minute session is just not going to get you anywhere close to this sort of experience." You will gain a little insight, a big toe in the waters but why dip and paddle when you can dive and experience total immersion. "Such a great way to journey – you can travel so far."

Clinical sex, just fucking, and not feeling, in our society seems to be strangely acceptable in our society, It is straightforward and closed. Sex is no longer a taboo. It is everywhere and it is used to sell anything and everything. "But pleasure is a taboo for when you are really taking pleasure you are no longer in control." Control is an interesting issue. "How often are we openly invited to lose control? Truly loving, giving, exploring, pleasuring and feeling pleasure is about abandonment. I am going to abandon myself, abandon myself to my desire, abandon myself to my partner, abandon myself to life, abandon myself to the real world. When you are really taking pleasure you are not in control." To relinquish your limitations is frightening. This is the pleasure taboo and Betony seeks to dismantle it. This is one of the reasons why pornography is so detrimental to our well-being and to our sex lives. "We are bombarded with a virtual reality, which seduces the desire centers within the brain because they are visually stimulated through the images on the screen." But this looking at the screen creates a physical detachment. The difficulties arise therefore because the visual desire centre can become so stimulated that the actual connected physical act is no longer of interest. You become unable to create your own reality, which 'sees' and feels through the experience of touch, taste, warmth and scent. Betony points out that "so many couples today are in a state of crisis because they are not acting on their own desires they are 're-acting' to the desires of someone else. And they find themselves disillusioned because their wife doesn't look like the chick who has more prosthetic material in her body than bones."

Betony is not anti-porn but she is an advocate of "stimulating the visual desire centers in a way that bridges the passage between having a desire and making that desire a reality. Turn off the porn and install some mirrors and get in front of them." She wants and encourages the creation of our own scenarios and not the mimicking of another's. "Take the time to create a sacred sexual space where you connect with yourself, and with your partner, not only physically, but emotionally and spiritually. When you have truly bonded, it will affect your energy fields and you will both radiate. The sexual union makes the spirit bloom; to ignore this is unhealthy. I encourage lovers to bring the sacred back into daily life, and this includes our sex lives."

"It is of tremendous importance, therefore, that we continue to attend and tend to our pleasures even when we are not in a relationship or with a lover. Masturbation is the essence of self-loving. It prevents the libido from going to sleep and the genitals for loosing their tonicity. The genitals need to be exercised and oxygenated regularly in order to remain in perfect health. There is no better way to keep them toned, fine- tuned and ready for action than sex - solo or shared."

Naturally our conversation broadens to the boom that is taking place in the vibrator industry. "Here we have to question what is being communicated when objects for adult pleasure assume toy-like aesthetics that are more likely to appeal to children that sexually mature adults; the alien, the dolphin, the bunny rabbit? Women's pleasure has being infantilized and it speaks volumes about the repression of a mature full-blown female sexuality." Hence Betony refers to her creations as tools or the implements of desire and not 'toys'. Hers are instruments for building desire. They increment our pleasures, not only physically but aesthetically as well. "I personally don't want a plastic bunny rabbit on my clit, I want a nice warm tongue and lots of lovely fingertips –in combination with one of my sterling silver dildos once things have been turned up a notch. I privilige making love to another, not to a machine."

Betony is astonished by the number of machines that are purely for clitoral stimulation. She is far from being against vibrators, far from it. As a tool they serve their purpose very well and one can, as she says "gasm" in a moment as they quite literally hit the spot. But these 'gadgets', and they are packaged as such, "appeal to a disempowered , un-evolved sexuality and our sexuality merits greater attention." Not only are these clitoral stimulators very clinical, in as much as they remain on the exterior of the body. They are not designed to enter into us. "The clitoral system is made up of more nerve cells than any other part of the body, male or female and the 'button' is quite literally the tip of the iceberg. So let us 'go in' and stimulate the organ as a whole - the female sexual 'apparati' is astonishingly filled with potential."

Betony Vernon's Paradise Found collection is about full body stimulation. She encourages us to erotically explore the whole body; treating our entire physical form as a sexual organ. "We need to open up the horizons of possibility, redefine normalcy, and stop putting limits everywhere." This is where Betony's motivations and interests lie and it is why she encourages and promotes a sexually creative relationship. The Paradise Found jewels therefore became a beautiful and seductive bridge in her mission to "…empower men and women to fulfill their innate desire to attain and provide greater sexual pleasure."

"Our misunderstandings are many; one person's pain is another person's pleasure... Just because you like to be restrained erotically does not mean quote unquote you are a sadomo-sochist... it is about breaking boundaries." But, she says, there is a desperate need to break down categories and bring initiation into this realm and goes on to describe a very real scenario. "Today you can go online and buy some potentially very extreme tools. Let's say it is a fine leather strap whip. I am feeling adventurous and my wife thinks a bit of flagellation might be interesting to try. I get out the whip, but there are no instructions with this potentially very dangerous object. It would be like being given an electric knife for your gourmet kitchen without any instructions. Potentially it could be very dangerous indeed. So we need to speak about initiation, the 'no-zones'. Let's talk about where I can strike, how can I strike, when I can augment the power of my strike, how can I make this tool work? Or lessen up? Otherwise it can be very dangerous, right?"

It is important therefore to know what these tools can do and how to use them because "it is not just about tantalizing the body, striking the body, penetrating the body and stimulating the body. You are also dealing with someone's emotions. It is a body, but it is a mind and it is a spirit too. So you have to understand your lover, their limits and you have to respect these. The goal, after all, is pleasure and with initiation and guidance you can really open up the horizons. Pleasure is subjective, just like one's threshold for pain—and our limits, no matter what they are, should be pushed skillfully in order that we provide pleasure and pleasure alone, especially where tools are concerned."

Paradise Found started as a collection of 70 pieces to what is now around 250 pieces. Created using the most beautiful of materials; silver, gold, wood and leather. Materials that all resonate and connect with the body. "Our bodies, after all warrant and deserve something beautiful, something natural and body safe." Betony firmly believes beauty is a symbol of respect. "There is beauty within all of us and we need to let that shine." The very nature of the beauty within her pieces is powerfully disarming and, in the process of being seduced by their beauty, she taps into our innate desires, which are often suffocated. There is an exquisite duplicity with her jewelry pieces. The objects live, or have a life, in the first place because Betony only works and creates with materials that speak, absorb energy and are in syntax with our bodies. She also seeks to empower the wearer. "When you wear one of my pieces, for example The Massage Ring, you know what it can do, and you also know that it can do something that your hands alone cannot do. So you head out into the world and you take with you, and hold, the power to provide plea-sure. You are aware of it and there is something joyful and beautiful in that." The Tickler Rings combine beautiful plumes with silver, passing as "full-on glamour pussy moments." But where the piece's true beauty and wonder lies is in the surprising juxtaposition of materials combined with the erotic potential to tickle and caress. "It serves as a reminder of what has taken place or of what is yet to come. This experience em-powers you because you are transporting that loving energy through the object and you carry it with you."

Desire is both implicit and explicit in Betony Vernon's creations. "My goal is to keep everybody's desire forces charged for when we nourish ourselves, our pleasures, and allow our desires to manifest, we are empowered. We are ready to take it on. We are ready to get lost and we are ready to have fun. So many people forget that sex should be fun. And the imagi-nation is such a critical part in this journey." The moment that your imagination is shut down is the moment that your desires become inflicted. Many would believe that Betony is focused on sex as a singular entity but this is far from the truth. She constantly refers and speaks of the spirit, of love, of emotion, of sharing and of feeling which is surely what we need and desire most in this world. "Our sexual well-being is crucial to our over all well-being; for our physical selves and our spiritual development and understanding. It is all intercon-nected." It is why The Petting Ring is such a key piece in the Paradise Found collection and probably best communicates Betony's vision and mission. The ring holds the index finger and thumb in the perfect 'chi mudra' position. This is the gesture used to assist in meditation, keeping oneself present and centered and in the moment. "When you slide on this ring it immediately aligns your energy. Yet, with a twist of the hand the ring becomes a beautiful yet powerful imple-ment of pleasure." We all have desires and they are so much part of what it is to be human. "Acting on our desires rather repressing them is the most fundamental thing that we can do for ourselves." Betony Vernon is certainly not talking about wreck-less sex and screwing anything that moves. Rather she speaks about the wonder of being wreck-less with someone you care about or love, with someone that you adore. "Desire needs to be fed and it needs to be nourished." Desire is about the wonder of bodies meeting, exploring and merging and being open to the possibilities that lie within; our ability to release ourselves and to abandon ourselves to each other, and to abandon ourselves to pleasure.

Betony passionately encourages lovers to learn to "fly high on our bodies natural love drug—endorphins. Lets learn to explore the body as a whole, to break down categories and to set the imagination and each other free." She invites lovers to go and make love, to loose their selves in the moment, and to "make a hot, wet, beautiful mess."

A/W 2011 by Charlie le Mindu.
Human hair, pvc and lace

'Fab' by Rebecca Wilson. Photographic series documenting the demise of a 'china' figurine cast in ice cream and chocolate in the style of the classic 'Fab' ice-lolly

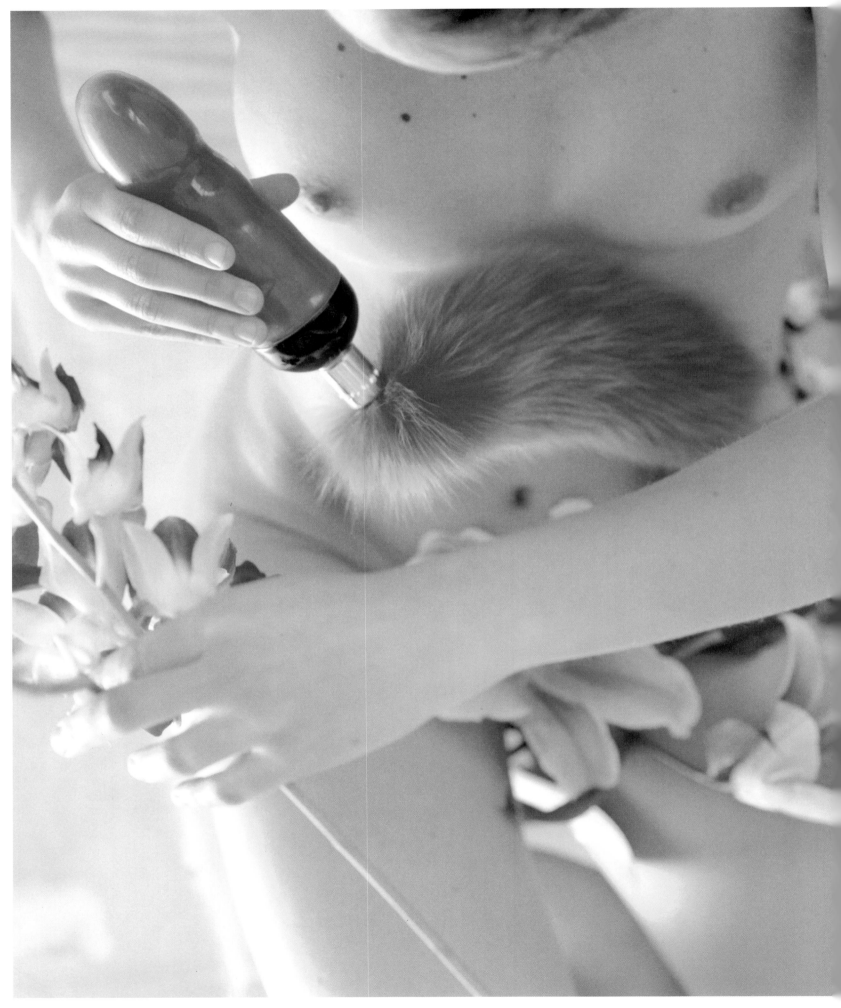

'Red Minx' by Shiri Zinn. Glass, Swarovski crystals and marabou feathers

'Fig': "No greater thing is created suddenly, any more than a bunch of grapes
or a fig. If you tell me that you desire
a fig, I answer you that there must be
time. Let it first blossom, then bear
fruit, then ripen." –Epictetus

'Pomegranate': *"and the pomegranates* –Oscar Wilde.
split and cracked with the heat, and A House of Pomegranates
showed their bleeding red hearts"

'Dream Topping' by Rebecca Wilson
2011. Porcelain

'Macaroons' by Ladurée. These small, round cakes, crisp on the outside, smooth and soft in the middle, are made every morning in Ladurée's *"laboratory."* The pastry chefs measure out very precisely the required amounts of almonds, eggs and sugar, before adding one final ingredient, a pinch of unique *"know-how,"* essential to the making of such a delicacy. Once cooked and filled, the macaroons are put to one side for 2 days before going

on sale, the time it takes to achieve
a perfect balance between texture
and flavour."

Baby criollo cocoa pod coddled between two adult cocoa pods on the community cocoa plantation in Cuyagua, Venezuela

Opposite page: Cocoa pods after harvesting. Cocoa pods come in a wide variety of different colors and shapes creating an almost

magical rainbow of color on the plantation.

ART POLLARD FROM AMANO CHOCOLATE
– CHOCOLATE QUESTIONS.

WHY IS CHOCOLATE AND COCOA SO CONNECTED TO DESIRE AND SENSUALITY? When we think of food and desire, there are few foods that spring to mind to the same degree as chocolate does. Since the time of the Mayans 2000 years ago, cocoa beans have been highly prized for their use in currency. These drinks that were also believed to enhance the virility of the ancient rulers. The Aztec ruler Montezuma was reported to have drunk over 50 cups of hot chocolate per day in cups made of gold or jewel encrusted shells. Since the time of Cortez the rest of the world has become obsessed with chocolate. The human soul of each person who comes in contact with chocolate is forever after obsessed with chocolate's magical flavor.

This obsession with chocolate has led to wars being fought, land possessed, and passions ignited. Pirates smuggled cocoa throughout the Caribbean, and villages ransacked -- the very things that are the making of myths. Today, chocolate is at the center of modern day legends, loves made and loves lost. Couples find each other, have children, grow old in each other's embrace. Chocolate is at the heart of each and every birthday, Christmas, holiday, birth and death until they too become the stuff of legend.

WHY IS IT SUCH A DESIRABLE FOOD? FIRSTLY FROM THE DELECTABLE TASTE TO THE EFFECTS IT HAS ON THE BODY AND TO OUR STATE OF WELL-BEING? Chocolate is less of a "flavor" and more of an experience. As chocolate melts in your mouth, it provides the rich textural contrast between the hard center, the soft melting surface, and the melted chocolate that is awash in flavor. The flavor of the chocolate is in itself a study in contrasts of flavor. There are over 1,500 identified flavor compounds in chocolate -- three times more than that found in wine. Some of these compounds are found naturally in the bean, some are developed as the freshly harvested bean is fermented and then sun dried, and others when the cocoa is roasted and turned into chocolate. The flavor of the chocolate is not like that of other sweets. It isn't fruity or spicy like cinnamon or peppermint, it is savory. This is why chocolate and cocoa make such a wonderful addition to chili's and stews. It is, I believe, this combination of incredibly complex savory flavors combined with the sweet sugar that I believe is at the heart of chocolate's intoxicating flavor.

WHY IS A HIGH QUALITY DARK CHOCOLATE SO GOOD FOR US? Good quality dark chocolate is an amazing food. It is in fact healtheir than many fruits and vegetables. How can something so sweet and delicious, such as chocolate be so healthy? Most fruits and vegetables have sugar in them naturally. In fact, most fruits and vegetables are chock full of sugar. Carrots are full of sugar as are beets, celery, and tomatoes. Cocoa beans naturally contain less than one percent sugar and while chocolate has sugar added, many times, fine quality dark chocolate contains less sugar than vegetables (not counting the vegetable's weight in water). Chocolate also contains extremely high levels of antioxidants, protein, fiber and has many nutritious minerals such as potassium, iron, magnesium, phosphorus, and copper.

Life expectancy is also tied to happiness. Studies show that happy people tend to live longer than those who are not happy with their lives, friendships and families. Chocolate also contains mood enhancers such as caffeine, theobromine and phenylethylamine and has been shown to boost seratonin. Seratonin is the chemical in our brains that is released when we are happy and in love. By eating chocolate, we have better odds of having a long and happy life. And if we don't, we will at least die happy.

WHY SHOULD WE EAT IT? There is only one true reason why we should eat chocolate. We should eat chocolate because it touches our soul. Yes, we can talk about how it is healthy for us but a vitamin pill is healthy. We could eat it because of its incredible texture, but many foods are fun in our mouths. We could eat it because it tastes good. There are many foods that taste good. In fact, there are many foods that taste very good. Chocolate transcends healthy, texture, or flavor. When you think about it, many foods are magical but none truly speaks to our soul in the way that chocolate does.

Cocoa beans being ground in a late
1930's vintage German melangeur.
The stone grinding wheels weigh over
1,300 pounds each. No longer made,
melangeurs slowly grind cocoa beans
into beautifully smooth chocolate

'Dirty Rotten Peaches'
by Rebecca Wilson 2011. Porcelain
and gold luster

'The Milkmaid' by Studio OOOMS.
Delftblue ceramic ware

Opposite page: 'Iro/色'
by Midori © 2005. Photo and rope art

'Princess on the Pea' by Richard
Hutton for Llove Hotel Tokyo

'Crystal Rose' by Noritaka Tatehana.
Chimera S/S 2011. Red Swarovski,
gold studded sole and rose petals

'Cage Belt' by Fleet Ilya. Leather

Oyster. *"We are bound to our bodies like an oyster is to its shell."* Plato

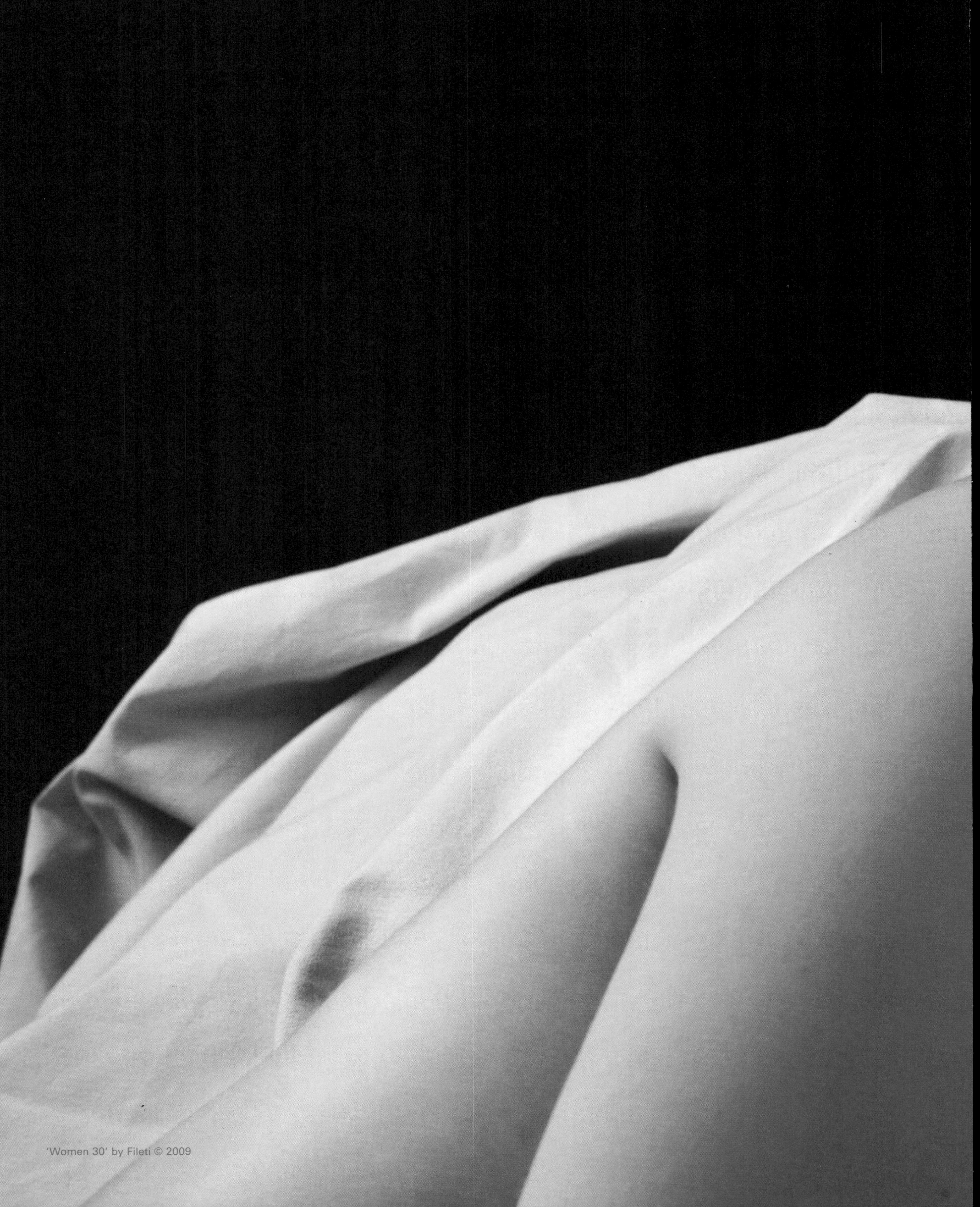

'Women 30' by Fileti © 2009

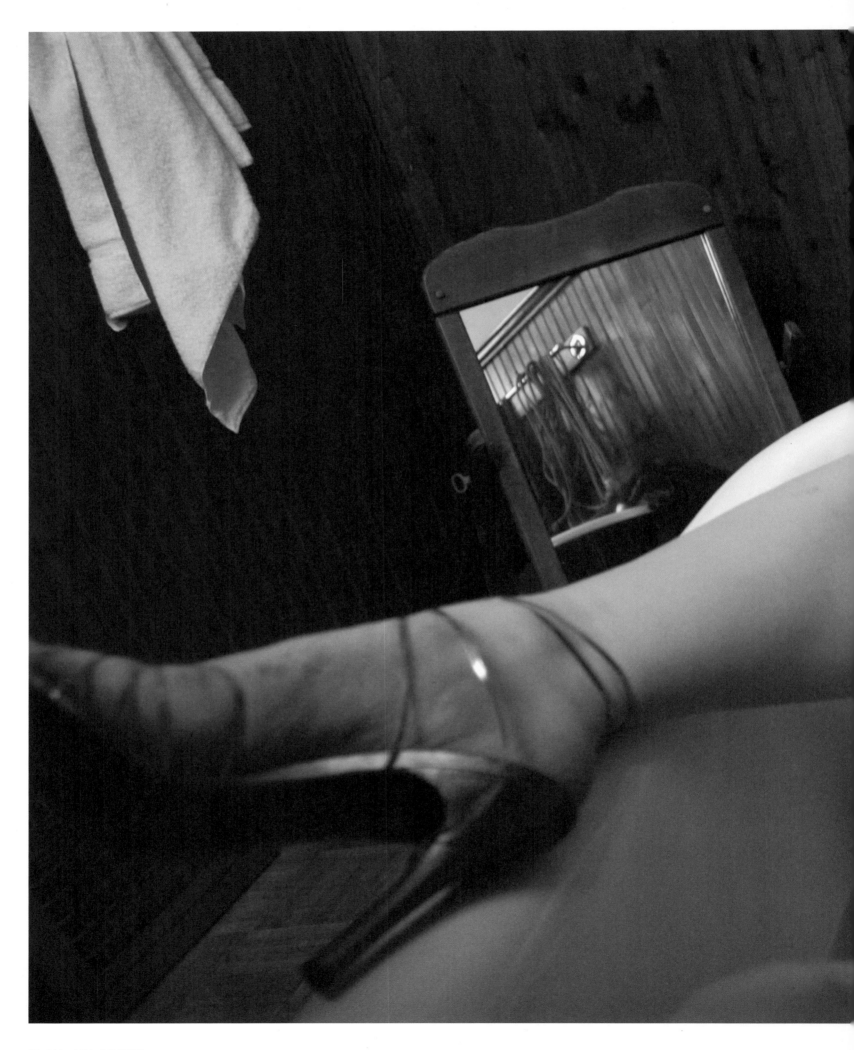

'Bath' by Midori © 2005.
Photo and Rope Art

'BB115' by Michael Petry 2010. Glass
and silver plated object. Collection
of Guy Burch & Richard Ayre at the
Sir John Soane's Museum, London

'Tartas' by Hans Gissinger 2005.
Image from 35mm film

"We never desire strongly, what we desire rationally"
—François de La Rochefoucauld

THE CURATED COLLECTION™

curator and author
LISA Z. MORGAN

creative direction and design
SUSANNE SCHAAL

editorial manager
NICKY STRINGFELLOW

book concept conceived by
PATRICE FARAMEH
LISA Z. MORGAN

we wish to thank all of the brands that participated in and submitted images and information for this luxurious book. any omissions for copy or credit are unintentional, and appropriate credit will be given in future editions if such copyright holders contact the publisher.

published + produced by
farameh media llc
217 thompson street
10012 new york city usa
p +1 646 807 1810
f +1 646 417 7999
info@faramehmedia.com

distributed worldwide by
daab media gmbh
scheidtweilerstr. 69
50933 cologne germany
p +49 221 690482 14
f +49 221 690482 29
mail@daab-media.com

PRINTED IN ITALY

ISBN 978-0-9830-8315-3